MW01104668

Lear's Daughters

American University Studies

Series XXVI
Theatre Arts

Vol. 29

PETER LANG
New York • Washington, D.C./Baltimore • Boston • Bern
Frankfurt am Main • Berlin • Brussels • Vienna • Canterbury

Rebecca B. Gauss

Lear's Daughters

The Studios of the
Moscow Art Theatre
1905–1927

PETER LANG
New York • Washington, D.C./Baltimore • Boston • Bern
Frankfurt am Main • Berlin • Brussels • Vienna • Canterbury

Library of Congress Cataloging-in-Publication Data

Gauss, Rebecca B.
Lear's daughters: the studios of the Moscow Art
Theatre 1905–1927 / Rebecca B. Gauss.
p. cm. — (American university studies.
Series xxvi, Theatre arts; vol. 29)
Includes bibliographical references and index.
1. Moskovskiĭ khudozhestvennyĭ akademicheskiĭ teatr—History.
2. Theater—Russia (Federation)—Moscow—History—
20th century. 3. Stanislavsky, Konstantin,
1863–1938. I. Title. II. Series.
PN2726.M62M655   792'.0947'3109041—dc21   98-33449
ISBN 0-8204-4155-4
ISSN 0899-9880

Die Deutsche Bibliothek-CIP-Einheitsaufnahme

Gauss, Rebecca B.:
Lear's daughters: the studios of the Moscow Art
Theatre 1905–1927 / Rebecca B. Gauss. –New York;
Washington, D.C./Baltimore; Boston; Bern; Frankfurt am Main;
Berlin; Brussels; Vienna; Canterbury: Lang.
(American university studies: Ser. 26,
Theatre arts; Vol. 29)
ISBN 0-8204-4155-4

Cover design by Nona Reuter

The paper in this book meets the guidelines for permanence and durability
of the Committee on Production Guidelines for Book Longevity
of the Council of Library Resources.

© 1999 Peter Lang Publishing, Inc., New York

Printed in the United States of America

To Emily, Elizabeth and Edward Gauss
whose contributions were too numerous to count

ACKNOWLEDGMENTS

I would like to thank the many people who contributed to the successful completion of this book. Thanks to M. Lee Potts, Merrill Lessley and James M. Symons at the University of Colorado at Boulder. Special thanks to C. Nicholas Lee whose help with my translations was invaluable as was his unfailing enthusiasm and encouragement. Thanks also to Regina Avrashov who never failed to help me in my struggles with the Russian language. Thanks to Masha Malkina, my excellent research assistant in Moscow as well as Sergei, Natasha, Dasha and Lyuba Ermish who fed and housed me during my time in Moscow and made me a part of their family. Thanks to Silverbrook Studios for its financial support and to Lena at the American Theatre Exchange Initiative for her logistical support in Moscow. Thanks also to Happy Schaffner for the many hours she spent proofreading. Finally and most profoundly I wish to thank Anatoly M. Smeliansky whose personal endorsement gave me access to the materials I needed and guaranteed the cooperation of the librarians. He found an assistant for me and spent many hours with me which he could ill afford. Without him, this book would have been nearly impossible and I am forever in his debt.

All photographs contained in this book are from the Moscow Art Theatre archive and are published with the permission of the Moscow Art Theatre.

CONTENTS

INTRODUCTION

When Tsar Peter the Great opened a window on Europe in the first years of the eighteenth century, he made it possible not only for Russians to know the rest of the world, but for the rest of the world to know the creative genius of the Russians. For the theatrical world, some of the most important work of that genius occurred in the first three decades of the twentieth century, before Josef Stalin closed Peter's window. By examining the role played by the studios of the Moscow Art Theatre during this important era, this book will attempt to clarify the many uncertainties surrounding them and to correctly attribute the contributions of the studios and their members to the reputation of the Moscow Art Theatre as an artistic and educational institution.

When Konstantin Sergeevich Stanislavsky and Vladimir Nemirovich-Danchenko founded the Moscow Art Theatre in 1897, they gave birth to a new age in Western theatre. The name of the Moscow Art Theatre soon came to represent the highest standards and greatest accomplishments in the theatre of its time, particularly among those theatres identified with the independent theatre movement. These accomplishments were not easily won, however.

In the spring and early summer of 1897, both Stanislavsky and Nemirovich-Danchenko felt compelled to take decisive steps toward the revitalization of a stagnant Russian theatrical scene. Stanislavsky, an amateur who had made a serious name for himself among theatre-goers, had decided to form his own professional theatre company. Nemirovich-Danchenko was a successful dramatist, two time winner of the Griboiedov prize for best play, and was heading the drama department of the Philharmonia School. When he learned of Stanislavsky's plans to form a company, it seemed prudent to investigate whether they could work together toward a common goal. Although the two men had never met, they were acquainted with each other by reputation. When Nemirovich invited Stanislavsky to join him for lunch at the Slavianskii Bazaar in order to discuss their common interests, Konstantin Sergeevich was quick to accept. The result of their conversation was the formation of the Moscow Art Theatre.

Stanislavsky and Nemirovich-Danchenko were men who had little in common outside of their theatre. Stanislavsky was a member of a wealthy industrialist family and Nemirovich, the son of a military man, earned his living with his pen. As Benedetti characterizes them,

> Stanislavski (*sic*) [was] a heavy smoker but otherwise abstemious, essentially puritanical in outlook, frowning on heavy drinking and extra-marital sex; Nemirovich [had] a taste for good living, for women other than his wife and for gambling.....Yet the two men came together as soul-mates, discovering complete unanimity in their dream of a new theatre (*Moscow Art Theatre Letters* 4).

Despite their spiritual affinity for each other as artists and visionaries, they disagreed on fundamental issues of theatre management and artistic priorities, a situation which would plague them throughout their long association.

The two men had different ideas about funding for their enterprise, Nemirovich expecting Stanislavsky to finance the theatre himself and Konstantin Sergeevich insisting on a public company with outside backers. Their early disagreements on this point were indicative of Nemirovich-Danchenko's basic distrust of the bourgeoisie and his fear of third parties. He resisted anyone who stood between himself and Stanislavsky, feared that aesthetics would be sacrificed to economics and attacked anyone who might influence Stanislavsky artistically. This attitude strained Nemirovich-Danchenko's relationships with his own former pupil Vsevelod Meyerhold, Stanislavsky's personal assistant, Leopold Sulerzhitskii, and Stanislavsky's talented and rebellious students, Evgenii Vakhtangov and Mikhail Chekhov (*Moscow Art Theatre Letters* 4–5).

While the structure of the theatre organization was often a source of argument, more important was their basic disagreement over the nature of theatre itself. Nemirovich, the playwright, saw theatre as a servant of literature, meant to provide a living illustration of the text. Stanislavsky, however, came to see the theatre as an art in its own right, demanding that playwrights see their text as part of a wider process which included the contributions of the actor and other artists.

Recognizing from the very beginning that they each had different talents to offer, the two decided on a division of power which worked for the first few years, but eventually failed. As originally planned, Nemirovich was to have veto rights on all literary matters while Stanislavsky had control on the production side. The difficulties arose when the two men could not agree on which area had priority. As the years passed, Nemirovich-Danchenko tried to gain control of all essential management decisions, then tried to control Stanislavsky's methods of working as a director. Although the Moscow Art Theatre was an international success, it was the cause of anxiety, discouragement, frustration and personal distress for its founders.

After seven years with the Moscow Art Theatre, Stanislavsky began once again to feel the need to explore new styles of production. He proposed the formation of a studio which was to be affiliated with the Moscow Art and dedicated to experimentation with space, design and acting style. This vision provided the primary through-line for all of the studios. It also fueled Nemirovich-Danchenko's opposition to them. Not only did he feel a studio setting was inappropriate for professional actors, he saw the studios as a distraction, drawing Stanislavsky's attention away from from the real work of the Moscow Art Theatre.

After the founding of that first studio in 1905, much of the groundbreaking work in acting, production practice and theatrical design which has been credited to the Moscow Art Theatre in the twentieth century was actually developed in the studio settings and not in the Moscow Art proper. It was in the studios that Stanislavsky refined his "system" of actor training. It was also in the studios that the directorial style of Evgenii Vakhtangov and the acting techniques of Mikhail Chekhov evolved.

There is, however, considerable confusion concerning the studios of the Moscow Art Theatre, especially in sources available in English. In many cases the contributions of the studios are overlooked or attributed to the Moscow Art Theatre itself. Distinctions between studios are vague and difficult to follow and conflicting dates are commonplace. Each studio was unique in its vision and its contributions and each enjoyed a period of creative autonomy which distinguished it both from the Moscow Art Theatre proper and the other studios. Most importantly, it was in the studios that Stanislavsky, his students and his colleagues experimented with exercises, ideas, philosophies and techniques which would be tried, rejected, re-worked and re-evaluated until they were finally formulated into what is now known as the "Stanislavsky System."

In order to clarify the many uncertainties surrounding the studios and to correctly attribute the contributions of the studios and their members to the reputation of the Moscow Art Theatre, it is essential to establish a chronological delimitation from 1905–1927. It was during this period, before the rise to power of Josef Stalin, that the studios emerged as the focus for innovative and creative theatrical work.

It is also necessary to define which of the several studios are included in this book, and why. I will examine, therefore, those studios known as The Studio on Povarskaya, The First Studio, The Second Studio, and The Third Studio. Excluded are the Opera Studio as well as any studio founded after 1927 and any other educational activities of

The Moscow Art Theatre which were not contained within the above mentioned studios.

This distinction is central to the focus of the book since the included studios are most directly related to the work of Konstantin Stanislavsky and the development of his "System of Actor Training." The development of this "system" is the fundamental unifying element shared by the included studios and one of the most important factors of the international reputation of the Moscow Art Theatre as an artistic and educational institution.

The Opera Studio is excluded from this book because its focus and activities diverge from those of the included studios. The impetus for the formulation of the Opera Studio was not Stanislavsky's but rather was initiated by the administrators of the Bolshoi, or Great Moscow Opera company for the benefit of its performers.

The Opera administrators approached Stanislavsky and asked him to coach their singers in matters of operatic acting. The students of the Opera Studio attended lessons in the "system" but did not contribute to its formulation. Neither did they experiment with the "system" nor modify its exercises as did many members of the included studios. While Stanislavsky developed classes and exercises specific to the Opera Studio's needs, for the members of the Opera Studio, Stanislavsky's "system" was merely one more useful tool to be included with their other training in order to enhance their performances and not an entirely new way to approach their work. This different attitude toward the "system" coupled with the fact that the Opera Studio was never an official affiliate of the Moscow Art Theatre in the way the included studios were, provide the basis for its exclusion from this book.[1]

Within the chronological delimitation of the study is the Fourth Studio which is also excluded from this book because its purpose and contributions were quite different from those of the included studios. While the included studios, each in its own way, were dedicated to the development of new theatrical forms and the education of new actors, the Fourth Studio of the Moscow Art did neither of those things. The Fourth Studio was primarily an educational outreach program intended to educate the audience, not the actors.

Formed in 1918 by a group of Moscow Art Theatre actors, the Fourth Studio performed in factories and workers' clubs in Moscow and the surrounding area. Organized as a collective of actors, the group brought productions of the classics to those segments of the Russian public which had previously been excluded from the Moscow Art Theatre audience. The work of the Fourth Studio was far from innovative and while the members of the included studios were searching for new modes of expression, the Fourth Studio was returning to the acting styles of the past.

The ideological foundation of the Fourth Studio was a desire to create a new communal theatre which would bring to the broad masses a theatre to which they could closely relate. The leaders of the studio believed that the best way to accomplish their goals was to embrace realism. In reaction to the formalism sweeping Russian theatre, the Fourth Studio of the Moscow Art Theatre laid the foundation for what would become Socialist Realism. The group produced plays which extolled the virtues of the working class and ridiculed the recently deposed aristocracy.

When the reorganization of the Moscow Art and its Studios occurred in 1924, the Fourth Studio was of little concern to Stanislavsky and Nemirovich-Danchenko (*Moscow Art Theatre Letters* 324).[2] It continued to operate autonomously until, in 1927, some of its members finally split from the Moscow Art and their organization was renamed The Realistic Theatre.

The members of the Fourth Studio did not experiment either with the "system" or with new forms of performance. Their goal was to educate the masses on social and political issues, not to improve their own work and they left behind little of lasting value. Rudnitsky characterizes the members of the Fourth Studio as "ill-starred" and "dull" (*Russian and Soviet Theater* 267), and as such their contribution to the Moscow Art Theatre's reputation is of little or no interest and is, therefore, excluded from further consideration in this book.

This book is a historical study and as such is based heavily on archival and original material. These materials were gathered by myself in May and June of 1994 from the extensive library at the Theater Workers' Union in Moscow and fall primarily into two categories: contemporary newspaper and magazine accounts of the activities of the studios and their members and anecdotal accounts written by the studio members themselves. The appendices were given to me in Russian by Anatoly Smeliansky prior to their inclusion in his recent publication celebrating the 100 year anniversary of the Moscow Art Theatre. All photographs reproduced in this book were obtained from the Moscow Art Theatre Museum Archive and are published with the permission of the Moscow Art Theatre.

The bulk of the materials used in the preparation of this book are in Russian. Translations are my own, prepared with the assistance of Dr. C. Nicholas Lee of the Germanic and Slavic Languages Department at the University of Colorado, Boulder. For those translated materials which were originally written in Russian, I have, when possible, consulted the original Russian language document as well. Quotations taken from Russian language sources appear in English in the body of the text with the Russian text appearing in the endnotes for each chapter.

Bibliographic entries are in the language of publication, favoring English for translated materials.

It is important for the reader who is not familiar with Russian names to have a basic understanding of Russian naming practices. All Russians have three names: a given name, a patronymic based on their father's given name, and a family name. Furthermore, the Russian language, including names, is controlled by suffixes which denote gender and case. Therefore, patronymics, or "father names" and family names reflect gender, with the suffix *ovna* or *evna* denoting feminine and *ovich* or *evich* denoting masculine in the patronymic and the feminine ending *aya* or *aia* and masculine *y* or *ii* on family names.

Russians customarily address each other either by given name followed by patronymic or by family name alone unless they are on very familiar terms. For example, Stanislavsky's given name was Konstantin and his patronymic was Sergeevich after his father Sergei. He is often referred to as K. S. for Konstantin Sergeevich. His mother's given name was Elizaveta, her patronymic was Vasilievna for her father Vasilii and her family name was Alekseeva (Stanislavsky was a stage name adopted by K. S. Alekseev.)

Another common ending in Russian names is *ova* and *ov*. In the case of the playwright Chekhov, he was properly addressed as Anton Pavlovich (for his father, Pavel) Chekhov while his sister was Maria Pavlovna Chekhova. Very often in Russian documents, initials are substituted for the given name and patronymic.

The transliteration of Russian names and words will, in most cases, follow the Library of Congress system for transliteration of modern Russian with the diacritical marks omitted. Exceptions are names which are commonly used in English language documents and are familiar to most readers, the most prominent example of which is Stanislavsky which can be correctly transliterated either with a "y" or "ii." In this book I have chosen to transliterate Stanislavsky and Tolstoy with a "y" but Sulerzhitskii, which is less common in English language publications and less familiar to American readers, with "ii." Similarly, while the Library of Congress system stipulates the name Dostoevsky should be spelled without a "y" in the middle, in this book Dostoyevsky is spelled with the "y" in the middle because this form is commonly used in English language documents. The complete set of standards for transliteration can be found in *The Transliteration of Modern Russian for English-Language Publications* by J. Thomas Shaw.

Finally, the Julian (Old Style) Calendar was used in Russia until 1918. To convert Old Style dates to New Style (Gregorian Calendar) during the nineteenth century, add twelve days and add thirteen during the twentieth. In 1918, therefore, February 14 (New Style), immediately followed January 31 (Old Style).

CHAPTER ONE

The Studio on Povarskaya:
A Search for New Forms

"The Art theatre, itself, with its naturalistic playing is not, of course, the last word and does not think to stop frozen in one spot: the 'young' theatre equally with its founder must carry on the work and go further" (*Articles, Speeches, Conversations, Letters* 175).[1] With these words, Konstantin Stanislavsky addressed his company at the opening of what would be known as the Studio on Povarskaya. He had come to believe that realism and local color, as practiced in productions of the Moscow Art Theatre, had "lived their life and no longer interested the public." Following the death of Anton Chekhov in 1904, Stanislavsky had grown increasingly dissatisfied with the aesthetics of the Moscow Art Theatre. Despite his unsuccessful attempt to stage three short plays by Maeterlinck in 1904, Stanislavsky was still determined to find an approach to the world of symbolist drama. "The time for the unreal on the stage had arrived" (*My Life in Art* 434). The date was May 5, 1905.

The impetus for this studio had grown out of an earlier idea of Stanislavsky's which was first documented in a paper entitled, "A Project for Organizing a Corporation of Provincial Theatres." Written in February, 1904, this document explains Stanislavsky's vision of three companies which would tour provincial Russia, each with a repertoire of fifteen plays. He hoped that these travelling troupes, trained in the tradition of the Art Theatre, would raise the quality of performance available in the provincial theatres and spread the ideals of the Moscow Art Theatre throughout Russia. Within a year, this plan began to take shape.

During the course of this year, however, there were important changes made to the original plan. Most of these changes were initiated by the man Stanislavsky chose to implement the project: Vsevelod Meyerhold. Meyerhold's own vision went beyond the improvement of provincial theatres and included the search for new forms, specifically a desire to successfully interpret a Symbolist play on the stage, a desire shared by Stanislavsky. Rudnitsky refers to a long note written by Meyerhold entitled "Toward the New Dramatic Company Project at the Moscow Art Theatre." In it Meyerhold criticizes both the provincial theatres and the Moscow Art Theatre itself.

In this note, Meyerhold also envisions a "new troupe, young, bubbling with newborn energy," which he hoped would revive the theatre and "excite both audience and actors with its constant efforts to improve." He also asserts that "the new theater must not be imitative. It must strive at all costs to develop clear individuality, since only individual art is beautiful." Meyerhold was searching for "new means of representation for a new dramaturgy such as the theater has not had until now" (Rudnitsky 53–54). Eventually, this search completely overshadowed Stanislavsky's original plan.

Vsevolod Meyerhold began his professional theatrical career with a provincial company in Penza, the city in which he was born. In 1896 he was accepted as a second-year acting student at the Moscow Philharmonia where he studied under Vladimir Nemirovich-Danchenko. Then, in 1898, he was invited to join the original company of the Moscow Art Theatre. There he played eighteen roles, including Treplev in the new theatre's first production of Anton Chekhov's *Sea Gull* (*Чайка*), as well as Tusenbach in *Three Sisters* (*Три Сестры*). Meyerhold left the Moscow Art Theatre in 1902 when the company was reorganized and he was not invited to become a shareholder. It is important to note that, as Marjorie Hoover asserts, Meyerhold left the Moscow Art Theatre "more for practical and personal reasons than for differences of principle with its artistic tendencies" (22).

In the three years between leaving the Moscow Art Theatre and returning to direct the Studio on Povarskaya, Meyerhold directed as well as acted in a cooperative of young actors known as the New Drama Association where he staged 170 plays in two years.[2] During this time his debt to his Moscow Art Theatre training outweighed his differences with its management.

The repertoire of the New Drama Association, which included plays by Chekhov, Hauptmann, Ibsen, Gorky and Nemirovich-Danchenko, closely followed that of the Moscow Art Theatre. This group of actors strove to bring to the provincial towns of Kherson and Tbilisi,[3] in addition to the familiar repertoire, the latest works of contemporary dramatists, such as Hauptmann, Maeterlinck and Schnitzler. In staging these works, Meyerhold searched for new ways to "break the frame of realism" (Hoover 23). At the heart of this search was not a simple infatuation with formalistic devices, but rather the new literature which compelled a departure from realism. It was a departure which Stanislavsky, a decade after his successful forays into both the realism of Saxe-Meinengen and the lyricism of Chekhov, sought as well. This common vision, along with Meyerhold's experiences in the provinces led Stanislavsky to invite the younger man to join with him in his new venture.

Vera Verigina records in her memoires a story passed to her by Boris Konstantinovich Pronin, a young actor at the Moscow Art Theatre. Following a performance of *Julius Caesar*, Stanislavsky invited Pronin to join him for a meal. Their conversation turned to Stanislavsky's plans for the new provincial troupes. Konstantin Sergeevich asked young Pronin's opinion of possible directors for the project. Pronin responded that, whoever was chosen must be, "the most straightforward, the most respected, the most cultured, the most authoritative person".[4] Stanislavsky immediately thought of Prince Sherbatov.[5] Then, in the next minute exclaimed, "But this is horrible, he died last year." After considering and rejecting other possibilities, Konstantin Sergeevich said, "There is only one person—Vsevelod Meyerhold, but he is on bad terms with the theatre. All the same, I am going to send him a telegram with an invitation."[6] In reply, Meyerhold wrote that he agreed with the principles of the venture and would come to Moscow in the end of April (68–69).

During the planning stages of the studio, Stanislavsky was concerned not only with directors, but with facilities as well. He became interested in what was formerly the Nemchinovsky Theatre on Povarskaya Street[7] and Merzlyakovski Lane. Located over a pharmacy, this small facility had been built originally as a serf theatre. The first auditorium was square, following the shape of the pharmacy, but was later enlarged and made more circular. The seating area included a lower level or "pit," a row of boxes, and a balcony. There was also a small foyer where, occasionally, dances were held following a performance. In its final configuration, the "pit" contained 537 seats in 27 rows and the balcony held 126 seats in 6 rows for a total of 663 seats. The auditorium also contained three large windows which overlooked Merzlyakovski Lane.

Upon close inspection, Stanislavsky found the facilities to be less than perfect. It was necessary to enlarge the stage, rearrange the dressing rooms and artists' lounge and build areas for set and prop construction. Stanislavsky offered to pay only 9,000 rubles per year, a sum to which the owners, a widowed millionaire named Titova and her son, did not immediately agree. Finally, on May 19, 1905, a two year lease was signed (Popov in *About Stanislavsky* [*О Станиславском*] 338–339).

During the summer of 1905, considerable remodeling was done at the theatre. This activity was not without its difficulties, many of which were aggravated by city bureaucrats in a newly organized building department who, without apparent malice yet quite effectively, hindered the process. For this reason, rehearsals could not be held in the theatre and the decision was made to move the company to Pushkino for the summer. Here, in the surroundings which had been so conducive to the creation of the Moscow Art Theatre in 1898, the actors, directors and designers could pursue their art, free of the distractions inherent in the remodeling project.

When the studio officially opened on May 5, 1905, Konstantin Sergeevich addressed the company of young actors, designers and musicians in a speech which, in hindsight, indicated the areas of friction which would emerge between Stanislavsky and Meyerhold as they moved through the rehearsal period. In his speech, Stanislavsky said:

> At the present time of the awakening of the social forces in this country, the theatre cannot, and has not the right, to serve only pure art—it must respond to social moods, to clarify them for the public, be the teacher of society. Furthermore, while not forgetting about its lofty social calling, the "young" theatre must at the same time strive towards the realization of its most important work—the renovation of dramatic performance (*Articles, Speeches, Conversations and Letters* 175).[8]

As time passed and rehearsals progressed, it became apparent that Stanislavsky's vision of the theatre as a social educator conflicted with Meyerhold's concepts. The young director expressed his own vision when he said, "How fine it is to laugh in the face of the crowd when it fails to understand us. The schismatic hermitage in the wilderness should light its beacon fire forthwith" (qtd. in Polyakova 172).

The Studio's repertoire was selected without friction, yet it "bore no relation to 'social moods' nor did it qualify the studio as 'society's mentor'" (Polyakova 172). The proposed repertoire consisted of both new pieces and old favorites from the Moscow Art Theatre. Included were *The Assumption of Hannele, Schluck and Jau* and *The Festival of Peace* by Hauptmann, Hofmannsthal's *The Woman at the Window*, Przybyszewski's *Snow, The Death of Tintagiles, Aglavaine and Selysette* and *Sister Beatrice* by Maeterlinck, Ibsen's *Love's Comedy* and Shakespeare's *Twelfth Night*. Plays by Verhaeren, Hamsun, Strindberg, Bryusov and Vyacheslav Ivanov were also slated for production. *The Death of Tintagiles, Love's Comedy, Snow* and *Schluck and Jau,* all directed by Meyerhold, and *Twelfth Night,* a reproduction of the Moscow Art Theatre staging under the direction of Burdjalov, were the first to begin rehearsal.

The actors for these productions were drawn from the Moscow Art Theatre school as well as other theatre schools in both Moscow and St. Petersburg, including the Alexandrinsky School. The company also employed some members of Meyerhold's New Drama Association. Included in the company were N. N. Volokhova, E. T. Zhikhareva, I. F. Kalitovich, O. I. Preobrazhenskaya, E. L. Shilovskaya, V. P. Verigina, Katie Munt (Meyerhold's sister-in-law,) V. F. Inskaya, V. A. Petrova, E. F. Safonova, O. P. Narbekova, A. V. Loginov, P. I. Leontiev, A. I. Kanin, Y. L. Rakitin, M. A. Betsky (also known as Kobetsky,) Samus (also known as V. V. Maximov,) I. N. Pevtsov, N. F. Kostromsky, A. P. Zonov and others. The directors were Meyerhold, G. S. Burdjalov, and V. E. Repman. B. K. Pronin and V. A. Podgorny served as Assistant Directors. The company artists were F. G. Golst, K. N. Sapunov, S. Y. Sudeikin, V. I. Denisov and N. P. Ulyanov. Ilya Satz composed the music for *The Death of Tintagiles*.

The administrative side of the Studio was made up of a board of directors who served without remuneration. These directors were Stanislavsky, Repman and S. A. Popov. Meyerhold also served on the board as a paid director. Savva Ivanovich Mamontov, a railway magnate and cousin by marriage to Stanislavsky, who spent a considerable amount of his fortune mounting theatrical and operatic performances, served as an unpaid special consultant.

As soon as the theatre was leased and it became clear that the company must go to Pushkino for the summer, it was also clear that Stanislavsky would not be present on a regular basis. Primarily, Konstantin Sergeevich feared that his presence would inhibit the creative work of the young artists. Secondly, poor health, with which he often struggled, drove him to travel to the spas at Essentuki and Kislovodsk. This situation did not indicate a loss of interest in the project, however. On the contrary, he stayed in close contact with both Meyerhold in Pushkino and his agents in Moscow. In this way he was able to remain informed and involved in both the production work and the theatre remodeling.

Pushkino, a small town in the countryside near Moscow, seemed both an ideal and an idyllic place for the actors and artists to work. The company lodged in cottages or *dachas* located between the streets of the town and the river. The young assistant director, Pronin, claimed one dacha for the "family of the princess" which then became known as "the family of Maeterlinckians," a reference to the importance of Maeterlinck's plays to the planned repertoire (Verigina 69).

Rehearsals were held in a nearby barn, located between the towns of Pushkino and Mamontovka. It was here that the search for new forms began to take shape. When rehearsals began for *The Death of Tintagiles*, Meyerhold first acquainted the actors with the verse of Maeterlinck.

Using a translation by Chulkov, Meyerhold compelled his actors to read the verse aloud, striving for limpid tones, a comfortable flow of words and pleasant breathing sounds, all the while struggling against their accustomed naturalistic style of reading.

Following these exercises, the company worked collectively using the original French text to improve on the translation. Then the actors read the verse both in French and in translation. Involved in this work were Shilovskaya, in the role of Igraine, Zhukhareva and Verigina playing Bellangere, Petrova and Munt as Tintagiles, Loginov and Rakitin playing Aglovale, and, as the Maids of the Court, Narbekova, Kolitovich, and Safonova.

In the book of collected essays entitled *Meetings with Meyerhold*, (*Встречи с Мейерхольдом*) Verigina characterizes Vsevolod Emelievich's rehearsals in the following, intriguing way. "Meyerhold's rehearsals were unusually absorbing and it was no less interesting and helpful to watch them than to be in the play" (32).[9]

At this early stage of his directing career, Meyerhold's enthusiasm about Symbolist dramas was irrepressible and inspired his staging of *The Death of Tintagiles*. His goal was to "inject the abstract imagery of Symbolism by the most energetic means into the reality of the Russian social struggle...he sought the 'dynamite' which was 'instantaneously' to destroy the old world" (Rudnitsky 58). This vision of the play had not yet evolved in 1905, but was clearly stated in the draft of an opening night speech for a subsequent production performed in Poltava in 1906. In the draft he wrote, "The island is 'our life,' the queen's castle 'our prison,' Tintagiles the embodiment of heroism and the pure idealism of champions of freedom, thousands of Tintagileses suffer in prisons and die. Our indignation must be directed against those responsible for their death" (qtd. in Rudnitsky 58). It was, in Rudnitsky's opinion, these early experiments with form which "determined in many respects the temper of all Russian Symbolist theater" (58). It was also during this time of experimentation that the differences between Meyerhold and Stanislavsky became evident.

In contrast to the Moscow Art Theatre's productions which attempted to show "pictures of life" on stage or the direct representation of the external world, Meyerhold strove to "represent and embody the relation-ship of the artist to the world and reality.... Meyerhold set himself the goal of realizing in the material concreteness of figures on stage the logic of the *imaginary and not the observed world*" (Rudnitsky 58-59). For the young director, Maeterlinck's play about fate and death became a symbol for the fatal incomprehensiblity of social existence.

Social and political issues were approached in a different manner at the Moscow Art Theatre than that which Meyerhold was attempting. Stanislavsky's position had always been that the theatre should be outside of the realm of politics. He believed that the theatre must be neither revolutionary nor reactionary, with the emphasis on aesthetics, hence the name "Art" theatre, and not on politics.

Meyerhold was also attempting to find a way to break with the naturalism of the Moscow Art Theatre productions by employing an elaborate stylization of speech. He wanted to use a disjointed speech structure to express the characters' sense of alienation and autonomy, an important element in Symbolist drama. "The internal connections in the dialogue were broken apart and it was turned in essence into a single monologue" (Rudnitsky 63–64).

While Stanislavsky agreed that such a step was needed, he soon realized that Meyerhold's approach was not the answer. What Konstantin Sergeevich experienced was essentially a rebellion of the "actor's theatre" against Meyerhold's new "director's theatre," an idea Vsevelod Emelievich further embraced after reading and translating some of the works of Gordon Craig. A similar rebellion would subsequently cause Vera Komissarzhevskaya to break with Meyerhold after he came to work at her theatre in St. Petersburg.

A clear example of Meyerhold's methodology is found in his director's notebook for *The Death of Tintagiles*. Referring to one point in the fourth act when the three Maids of the Court speak, Meyerhold describes the desired effect as simultaneous speech with one voice only occasionally rising above the others. At this moment, Meyerhold transformed the three characters into a chorus speaking a single monologue. The effect was such that, "Individual differences were unimportant and almost disappeared. What was shared resounded powerfully, spoken by three voices" (Rudnitsky 64).

Another description of what Meyerhold hoped to accomplish is found in a note, written on Studio stationery, which states:

> Maeterlinck.
> 1. Experience of the form, and not experience of single psychological emotions.
> 2. A smile for all.
> 3. Never tremolo.
> 4. Read lines as if there were hidden in every phrase a profound belief in an all-powerful force.
> 5. Firmness of tone, since blurring will make it sound "moderne."
> 6. Motionless theater.
> 7. Do not drag out the ends of words The sound should fall into a great depth. It should be clearly defined and not tremble in the air.
> 8. Like a piano. That is the reason for no vibration.
> 9. No speaking in a rapid patter. Epic calm.
> 10. Madonna-like movements (qtd. in Rudnitsky 64–65)

Nine of these ten points are aimed at the actors and six refer to the way they should speak. The sound of the production was clearly of great importance to the director. By fighting against tremolo and blurring of sound, seeking clear definition and epic calm, Meyerhold was asking the actors to work in complete opposition to the Moscow Art Theatre's pursuit of subtle, psychological interpretation of each character at any given moment.

The essence of Meyerhold's new approach depended heavily on the use of the actor's voice. Speech was no longer meant to illuminate the character's psychological state, as was the approach of the Moscow Art Theatre. Meyerhold sought the universal, rather than the personal or individual, and dictated "the tone, the resonance, the intonation for the whole production and all the actors, the rhythm of 'reading' obligatory for all" (Rudnitsky 65).

This use of the term "a reading" was new with Meyerhold and was in extreme contrast with the Moscow Art Theatre technique. The use of the clear sound of a piano as the example for the actors' tone was an innovation as well. These ideas, along with those of "motionless theater" and "bas-reliefs" as aesthetic characteristics for Symbolist productions would prove to be short-lived and unsatisfactory. Ultimately, at the insistence of Vera Komissarzhevskaya, Meyerhold would abandon this style of *mise-en-scene* for his productions.

Verigina relates one way in which Meyerhold's ephemeral vision was made concrete for the actors through the use of pauses and silence. She explains:

> Igraine, Bellangere, and Tintagiles communicated their emotions with a cold sound, but with it was a sensation of suppressed excitement, and all the emotion lay in the pause, which was the result of the highest tension of feelings. Where in naturalistic performance there would have been a shout, it was replaced by unexpected, intense silence (*Meetings with Meyerhold 33).*[10]

Such attention to silence and pauses, while not entirely unknown, was taken to greater lengths in *The Death of Tintagiles* than it had been in any previous productions.

The same careful attention was given to movement and gesture. Meyerhold's concept of "motionless theatre" was heavily influenced by early Russian primitives and religious icons. This connection seems natural when considered in conjunction with the attitude towards theatre which he held at that time. For Meyerhold, in 1905, the theatre was, "a cathedral of sorts in which actors were the priests and sacristans and the audience the believers" (Rudnitsky 64). In the hands of the young director, Maeterlinck's play became almost a ritual. The actors were given carefully choreographed movements and gestures to perform and were often posed with the inclined heads and soulful expressions commonly found in the iconography of Russian Orthodoxy.

To add a feeling of mystery and unreality to the careful choreography, the first act of *The Death of Tintagiles* was performed behind a scrim curtain. A backdrop representing the sea and the castle on the cliff was visible behind a row of "giant cypresses;" at downstage left was a small bridge; in the center a summerhouse; and at right, a hill. Meyerhold's notebook details the the first entrance of Tintagiles and his sister Ygraine.

> Tintagiles enters downstage on the hill B and Ygraine upstage. At the top of the hill Tintagiles pauses, kneels, and plucks a flower, a long-stemmed symmetrical lily growing at the top of the hill. Ygraine stands still. Bas-relief. Then they walk in the direction of the arrow in the sketch. For a time they disappear from view. They are hidden by the little hill D. Then they come into sight again. This time from the left on the little bridge A, Ygraine ahead, Tintagiles behind. They pause. Tintagiles lowers his arms over the railing. (He holds the flower in his hands—and continues to do so the whole time.) Ygraine has stopped and looks at him. Pause. Then they speak (qtd. in Rudnitsky 67).

In this manner Meyerhold carefully scored the action. This began what came to be known as "motionless theatre" or theatre of slow, significant, profound motions. In this style of performance, Meyerhold hoped to give an impression of motion in tune with the hidden spirituality of the play as opposed to a rendering of human motion in real life. The plasticity of human motion was subordinated to the rhythm of the play (Rudnitsky 66–67). With his concept of "Madonna-like movements" and close dictation of every move and pose, the play approached ritual.

It was not only in the areas of sound and movement that Meyerhold was reversing practices of the Moscow Art Theatre. He also made major changes in the methods used by the company's set designers. At the Moscow Art Theatre it had been the practice to build a detailed *maquette* or model of a proposed set design before any construction began. While it was in the model stage, Stanislavsky would carefully review and either accept, reject or change a design. For the Studio on Povarskaya, Meyerhold decided to forego the model stage, asking his young designers to produce sketches and drawings which would indicate the overall feeling of the setting without giving detailed plans. Although it has been suggested that two of his designers, Nikolai Sapunov and Sergei Sudeikin, were complete novices and did not know how to build a *maquette*, Meyerhold later indicated that the overriding reason for the procedural change was more central to the philosophy of the work. He likened the destruction of the maquette to the destruction of contemporary theatre practices. He "wanted to burn and stamp the models underfoot" and thereby burn "the outmoded methods of naturalistic theatre" (qtd. in Rudnitsky 66).

It must also be noted, however, that the nature of the plays, especially *The Death of Tintagiles*, dictated important changes in scenic practice. For example, a considerable amount of the action takes place in a medieval castle. If this castle were built realistically, scene changes would take more time than the acting, itself. For this reason it was necessary to devise a stylized castle. What resulted was a shift away from topography toward artistic representation. Furthermore, since the designers were also the artisans who painted the sets, detailed plans were less essential than if the job had to be passed on to others for execution.

In the move away from realism, the artists introduced the principles of impressionism to scenic art, using color to evoke mood and emotional effect. This did not mean, however, a total rejection of realism. Certainly there were realistic touches such as the sea-shore, the row of cypress trees and the castle. What was new and impressionistic was the fact that all of the sets for *The Death of Tintagiles* were painted in shades of blue-green.

A similar path was chosen for the production of *Schluk and Jau*. In this case, the settings were designed by Nikolai Ulyanov to give the impression of locale and period. Ulyanov, following the suggestion of Stanislavsky and inspired by an exhibition of historical portraits, moved Hauptman's play from the medieval period to the late eighteenth century. The first tableau was placed in front of an impression of grand palace gates and the second setting included a luxurious royal bed. The most impressive setting was the third which consisted of basket-like summerhouses stretched across the downstage area in which were seated the ladies of the court, all embroidering in unison a single broad ribbon.

Unlike Sapunov and Sudeikin, Ulyanov worked with a *maquette* which was seen by Stanislavsky before the set was built. Ulyanov relates that many such *maquettes* were built, destroyed, changed and rebuilt (197). Even though Stanislavsky was extremely occupied at this time, he did check with the young designer whenever possible and it was Stanislavsky who realized that the set as designed was too large for the small stage. Questions of scale, however, were realtively insignificant and much more easily remedied than the looming stylistic and aesthetic conflicts. What later came to be one of the biggest disappointments with the Studio was linked to the fact that no one, including Stanislavsky, was able to anticipate the final result when Meyerhold's new style of acting was placed in the sets as designed and built.

In *My Life in Art*, Stanislavsky writes about the first time the work of the Studio was shown. In August he, along with Savva Mamontov, playwright Maxim Gorky, and several actors and designers from the

Moscow Art Theatre, traveled to Pushkino to see rehearsals of the works in progress. The pieces presented for him were *The Death of Tintagiles*, *Schluck and Jau* and one act of Ibsen's *Love's Comedy* and the entire day, as Stanislavsky wrote to Popov, "made me very happy"(344).[11]

In the morning the young company presented *Schluck and Jau*. Stanislavsky found the work to be "fresh, youthful, inexperienced, original and appealing" (qtd in Polyakova 176). The afternoon was spent playing tennis and Russian skittles followed by dinner on the terrace. Then, in the evening, the company presented *Love's Comedy* and *The Death of Tintagiles*. It was the latter which made the greatest impression or, as Stanislavsky wrote to Popov, "caused a furor"(344).[12] To his wife, Stanislavsky characterized *The Death of Tintagiles* as "Spectacular. It is so lovely, so new, so sensational" (qtd. in Polyakova 176).

In contrast, the showing of *Love's Comedy* was not as well received. Stanislavsky was optimistic, nevertheless. He wrote to Popov:

> "Love's Comedy" has been an indifferent success, but I think I have understood why and will be able to give good advice. The most important thing was that yesterday it became clear: We have a troupe, or more accurately, good material for one. This question tormented me all summer, and yesterday I regained my composure. Yesterday the pessimists began to believe in the success of the Studio and acknowledged its first victory (344).[13]

With feelings of satisfaction, joy and anticipation, Stanislavsky left Pushkino and returned to Moscow.

During the time that Meyerhold was shaping the Studio in Pushkino, Popov and the young designers were remodeling and refurbishing the theatre on Povarskaya Street. The auditorium was the source of many difficulties and disagreements. Contrary to what was common in theatre architecture, the auditorium was not located in the center of the building but along the facade. This meant that the noise from the street was a serious factor. It was decided that the addition of heavy draperies on the windows would provide at least a partial solution.

Another difficulty with the auditorium was the floor. As originally built the floor did not slope, a feature deemed essential by those in charge of the renovation. The estimated cost to rebuild the floor into a conventional rake was 600 rubles and a week's time. When approached about this situation, Stanislavsky replied in a letter to Popov which reveals the frustrations inherent in the project.

Konstantin Sergeevich was impatient with the renovations and wanted to concern himself with art, not architecture. He was also concerned about the time necessary to change the floor. In the letter he pointed out that, while the job itself might cost 600 rubles, when considered in light of the delay it would cause in opening the theatre, the cost increased to 4550 rubles. Stanislavsky, furthermore, did not want to think about the floor when there were serious artistic questions occupying his thoughts. In his opinion, if the production is good, the floor is inconsequential and, conversely, if the production is poor, changing the floor will not fix it. In the final analysis, he left the decision of whether or not to rake the floor to Popov's discretion with the admonition, "I do not go against the general opinion, but ask only that you weigh all questions asked and evaluate them, in terms of what is more important now: in every possible way to hurry the artistic work or occupy yourself with the floor" (qtd. in Popov 340).[14]

Another difficulty with the auditorium was the seating arrangement. Instead of individual chairs, the theatre was equipped with small divans which seated four people. Originally, those in charge of the renovation thought that new seating should be purchased. After many meetings devoted only to questions of seating and the floor, it was decided that a better solution was for the Studio's propmaster, V. E. Egorov, to repair and refurbish the divans. In the end, these divans outlived the Studio (Popov 340).

Greater attention was given to the other public parts of the theatre, especially the foyers and refreshment area. The desire was to create something new, youthful, and unlike any other theatre. Much of this work was left to the Studio's young artists, particularly Sapunov, Sudeikin, Ulyanov and Goltz.

The general concept was to create a place which personified the name "Theatre Studio." The choice of the word "studio" had been Meyerhold's originally and was meant to signify an institution somewhere between a professional theatre and a school. This distinction was one that would continue to be debated as other studios were formed and re-formed. It was of particular interest to Nemirovich-Danchenko who always asserted that a professional theatre, such as the Moscow Art Theatre, could not do experimental work and students in a school are not yet ready to experiment. Therefore, the Studio on Povarskaya and the other studios which followed were the domain of those students who had completed a certain degree of study but were not yet fully professionals.

The plan for the facilities on Povarskaya was an attempt to reflect the work of the young artists and give the impression of a club for actors and artists. Sudeikin, under the influence of a recent trip to Italy, created a room reminiscent of Venice. Sapunov and a young sculptor named Bramirsky worked together on a corridor while Goltz concentrated on the refreshment area and Ulyanov refurbished the oval foyer in a style reminiscent of a garden. The foyer included large vases of live flowers and an oversized oval table with art journals displayed on it. Another foyer was painted sky-blue and the third was white. In the refreshment area the ceiling was painted with masses of forget-me-nots and plans were made for the waitresses to wear white and sky-blue dresses with beribboned caps.

During this process of refurbishing the public areas, a floor once again became a point of contention. Ulyanov thought it would be a good idea to paint the parquet floor in the main foyer green, reminiscent of beautiful Russian malachite. The young artist believed his paint job had the charm of lovely, old marble, but Stanislavsky perceived it otherwise. As soon as he saw the floor, he stopped in his tracks, set his shoulders and sternly requested that by the next day the floor be returned to its original appearance. All through the night the artist, along with carpenters and other workers, labored on the floor and by morning it had been returned to its original state. Despite this difference of opinion, Ulyanov characterizes Stanislavsky as extremely supportive of and enthusiastic about the work of the young artists (199).

As summer ended and autumn began, the theatre building approached readiness and the troupe returned to Moscow from Pushkino. While the Studio members were anticipating their opening and the changes it would bring to the theatre, major social and political changes took center stage.

October of 1905 saw the culmination of years of social unrest in Russia. A general strike began in Moscow and theatres were closed as water was cut off and power failed. On October 18 Nikolai Bauman, a Bolshevik revolutionary, was killed in the street by the Tsar's secret police. His funeral, on October 20, became an enormous left-wing demonstration. Many Moscow intellectuals, including members of both the Art Theatre and the Studio, were drawn into the conflict and even Stanislavsky himself signed a petition protesting Bauman's murder.

In the midst of the turmoil, the Studio was attempting to ready its productions for public performance. The opening date was repeatedly pushed back, however. Finally a general rehearsal was scheduled and the company prepared to show its work to Stanislavsky and the Moscow Art Theatre community. What followed verged on disaster.

Vera Verigina indicated where some of the difficulties lay, particularly in regards to the musical scoring. She believed that the composer, Ilya Satz, had failed to catch "the rhythm and intonation of the actors" (qtd. in Rudnitsky 69). Verigina acknowledged that the conflict between performers and composer was due both to uncertainty on the part of the former and the inexperience of the latter. The end result, however, was that Satz had written music to express his personal interpretation of Maeterlinck's play which did not coincide with that of the overall production. Certainly, Satz's music was a strong contributor to the production's shortcomings. Meyerhold had envisioned that the entire play should be underscored, but the end result was that the music overpowered the acting.

In retrospect, however, the experiment was not without its positive points. It was actually a ground-breaking attempt to change the nature of theatrical music and was, in many ways, a bold and innovative step. Satz approached his composition, not as illustration of the action on stage but as a foundation upon which the production would be built. He also sought new ways to use the instruments of the orchestra in order to present sounds appropriate to the play and unlike those commonly heard in the opera or the concert hall (Varpakhovsky 7–10).

Another disappointment was the completed sets. Verigina records that the designers' work was quite beautiful in itself but, like the music, overwhelmed the production. At the general rehearsal it became clear that the plain canvas background which had been used for rehearsals was actually more effective than was the elaborate set as it allowed gestures to be more sharply outlined and clearly defined. Furthermore, Sudeikin's inexperience as a lighting designer created yet more difficulties. His use of color became problemmatic when his blue-green lighting "changed the color, and drowned and blurred the figures of the characters; their hair and faces took on unexpected shades" (qtd. in Rudnitsky 69).

According to S. A. Popov, Verigina's perception of the problem corresponded exactly to that of Stanislavsky and Nikolai Ulyanov's recollection of the general rehearsal has become an almost legendary anecdote.

> Semi-darkness on stage. Only people's silhouettes are visible. The set is flat, without wings, and hung almost at the footlights. This is new, and also new is the way the actors' rhythmic speech is projected from the stage. The action develops slowly; it seems as if time has stopped. Suddenly a shout from Stanislavsky: "Light!" a tremor is felt in the theatre, noise, confusion. Sudeikin and Sapunov jump up from their places, protesting. Stanislavsky's voice: "The audience cannot take darkness on the stage for long, it goes against psychology, they must see the actors' faces!" Sudeikin and Sapunov: "But the set is made for semi-darkness, it makes no artistic sense in the light!" Again there is silence, with only the beat of the actors' measured speech, but now the stage is fully lit. But no sooner have they turned on the light than the whole set is ruined. Divergence and discord has begun between the painting of the set and the figures of the characters in the play. Stanislavsky stands up, then the onlookers too. The rehearsal is interrupted, the production is not approved (201).[15]

Clearly Meyerhold had not achieved his goal of harmonizing the plastic form of "motionless theatre," the impressionistic sets, the music of the diction and the music of the orchestra into a unified whole.

The first showing of *Schluck and Jau* was only slightly more successful. One factor may have been Stanislavsky's greater participation in this piece, since he had spent some time working with the actors. He was especially helpful to the women, coaching them in the proper way to maneuver in their wide dresses and high wigs. Rudnitsky offers another possible explanation for the production's limited success, which is related directly to the nature of the play.

> Hauptmann's elegant "play of jokes and witticisms" was generously strewn with biting laughs at the ruler's power and at the flattering courtiers and jesters, etc. But apparently in this instance Meyerhold was not able to pursue any particularly serious ideological or political aims. The carnival game which animates the plot of the play was amusing and full of a lot of blunt jokes and puns. The people of the noble court with its princes, pages, banquets, tapestries, hunting horns, jesters, etc., allowed the imagination free rein. To a certain extent, work on *Schluck and Jau* evidently revealed the first possibilities of stylization, to which Meyerhold later devoted a great deal of energy. But for the time being, this was only a careful reconnoitering of new ways, and nothing more (71).

Unfortunately, this "reconnoitering of new ways" was not, in itself, enough for the production to succeed. As with *The Death of Tintagiles*, there was still a lack of harmony between the different elements of the production.

Ulyanov, as the designer of *Schluck and Jau*, remembers the showing in different terms than do other commentators. He offers a detailed description of the visual images of the play which were, perhaps, the most successful element of the production. While the opening scene, played against a background which suggested high, ornate gates, was well received, the greatest response came later, during the scene with the seven princesses.

> On the stage seven princesses are seated in seven trellised bowers, through which sparkles the sky with fleecy clouds. Off stage Gliere's music is heard. Across the whole length of the stage, seven princesses are embroidering a single golden ribbon, which stretches the whole length of the stage, and unites them compositionally. There is loud applause starting in the first rows, then throughout the whole theatre. I trembled. The applause was for me, the artist, who was displaying for the first time his powers in the realm of design. This encouraged me and it seemed to me that the concern of all the troupe about the future of the theatre was totally unwarranted and that everything would turn out as it should (202).[16]

It soon became clear that Ulyanov's predictions of success were premature.

Stanislavsky's assessment of the productions following the general rehearsal was far from optimistic. He realized that there was something fundamentally wrong with the entire process. He wrote:

It all became clear. The young inexperienced actors were capable of showing the audience their new experiments with the help of a talented director, but only in small excerpts. When it came to developing plays of tremendous inner content with delicate outline and, in addition, stylized form, the young people showed their childish helplessness. The talented director tried to protect actors who in his hands proved to be mere clay with which to mold beautiful groups and tableaux, and with whose help he realized his interesting ideas. But since his actors lacked artistic technique, he could only demonstrate his ideas, principles, searching, but had nothing or no one to realize them with. For this reason the interesting aims of the Studio turned into abstract theory, scientific formula. I was once again convinced that there is a great distance between a director's dreams and their realization and that theater exists first of all for the actor and cannot exist without him, and that for new art you need new actors with a completely new technique (qtd. in Rudnitsky 72).

As unrest brewed in the streets, the members of the Studio, as well as all the people of Russia, found it impossible to remain aloof or unconcerned. Even as he prepared for the Studio's opening, Stanislavsky struggled with philosophical and political questions. Ulyanov expressed the general concern when he asked, "Is it possible to open the theatre with a repertoire which does not respond to the mood of the masses?" (200).[17] As the bitter street fighting of the 1905 revolution overwhelmed Moscow, Stanislavsky made the decision to close the Studio.

In addition to artistic, philosophical, and political issues, money had become a problem as well. When they first discussed the project, Stanislavsky told Popov that money was not needed and that he, Stanislavsky, would pay the expenses. By October, when the Studio failed to open and there was no income in sight, the financial difficulties had become overwhelming.

Popov relates in detail the financial woes of the Studio. From the beginning, Stanislavsky was intent on financing the project himself. One donation of 700 rubles was made privately in June, but otherwise the burden was entirely Stanislavsky's. By September 21, he had paid out 9,900 rubles and owed nearly 35,000.

Konstantin Sergeevich had given Popov Power of Attorney which allowed him to complete transactions, conclude negotiations and gain credit in the name of Stanislavsky. Popov was reluctant to exercise this right, and since he had obtained some money by other means made a loan of 25,000 rubles to the Studio, which was, in reality, to Stanislavsky personally. By the end of September it was repaid. Finally, however, Stanislavsky resorted to pledging a share of the Alexeev business, not a simple matter in October of 1905 when the country was in turmoil. Ultimately, Popov loaned another 14,800 rubles on November 2.

By the time of this final loan, the situation was quite grim. The Studio was originally slated to open its season on October 1. This date was pushed back to October 10 and then delayed once again. On October 14 all the theatres in Moscow were closed.

When the project was begun, the name of Stanislavsky was of sufficient stature in both the business and theatrical communities to guarantee financial backing, should it be needed. The work of the Studio, however, was very new and it was necessary to have first a successful season in Moscow and then a success in the provinces for the Studio to become established. Popov believed that, had the social, political and financial state of Russia been more stable, the Studio could have survived. In the difficult conditions of October 1905, it was impossible.

The orchestra was paid and released at the end of the Christmas holidays. On May 1, 1906, the rest of the troupe was paid a full year's severance pay and the Studio was dissolved. Stanislavsky returned to his work at the Moscow Art Theatre and Meyerhold went to St. Petersburg to work for Vera Komissarzhevskaya in her new theatrical venture.

Some time later, Meyerhold summarized the Studio experience in the following way:

> For me it was a personal drama that Stanislavsky closed the studio on Povarskaya in 1905, but basically he was right. In my characteristic haste and heedlessness, I wanted there to bring together the most disparate elements: symbolist dramaturgy, artist-stylists and young actors, nurtured in the early school of the Art Theatre. Whatever the tasks I set myself, all of it failed to come together and, to put it crudely, was reminiscent of the fable of the Swan and the Pike. Stanislavsky, with his tact and taste, understood this, and for me, when I came to my senses after the disappointment of the fiasco, it taught me a lesson: first it is necessary to educate a new actor and then to put before him new tasks. The same conclusion had also been made by Stanislavsky, in whose mind even then the features of his "system" in its first edition were already ripening (*Stanislavsky* 71–72).[18]

This bitter viewpoint was in contrast to that of Stanislavsky himself. Although he had surely borne the brunt of the failure, personally and financially, he remained philosophical. From his standpoint, this first experiment in the renewal of theatrical art was a failure only in terms of finances. Even his artistic disagreements with Meyerhold had served the function of helping Stanislavsky to focus his work, moving him ever closer to his goal of creating a sharp, spiritual realism. The work on Povarskaya clearly showed Stanislavsky that, while he himself was interested in character, Meyerhold was interested in archetypes and for this reason, if for no other, they could not work in the same way.

In 1908 Stanislavsky wrote, in a report on the tenth anniversary of the Moscow Art Theatre, that "When artistic perspectives became cloudy, the Studio was born. It died, but for all that our theater found its future among its ruins" (qtd. in Rudnitsky 75). Indeed, the Studio on Povarskaya was merely the first episode in an extended period of experimentation and searching.

Konstantin Stanislavsky 1916

Meyerhold with Members of the Studio on Povarskaya 1905

Vsevelod Meyerhold 1902

CHAPTER TWO

The First Studio:
The Birth of the "System"

The failure of the Studio on Povarskaya Street was a great disappointment to Stanislavsky, but in no way did it end his interest in creating an environment for experimentation both in performance and actor training. During the years between 1905 and 1912 Konstantin Sergeevich continued to search for the keys to the actor's art which would unlock, for both the master and his students, the barriers which thwarted them in their search for truthful and free expression on the stage.

As the Moscow Art Theatre approached its fifteenth year of operation, its productions focused a great deal of attention on the psychological problems and questions of modern life, while at the same time performing primarily the classical repertoire of Russia and the West. Stanislavsky felt that the methods of the Moscow Art Theatre had become stale and tired and that there was no place on its stage for offerings of emerging or innovative work. He believed it was time to once again establish a place where experimentation could flourish.

As early as 1906 Stanislavsky had come to realize that he was no longer offering his audiences the inspired performances of his earlier career. He expresses his disillusionment with himself in *My Life in Art* in the following way:

> I wanted to find out where all my former joy in creation had vanished. Why was it that in the old days I was bored on the days when I did not act, and that now I was happy on the days I was free from work? It was said that it could not be different with a professional who played every day and who often repeated the same roles, but this explanation did not satisfy me.... Why was it

then that the more I repeated my roles the more I sunk backward into a stage of fossilization. Examining my past step by step, I came to see clearer and clearer that the inner content which was put into a role during its first creation and the inner content that was born in my soul with the passing of time were as far apart as the heaven and the earth....God, how my soul and my roles were disfigured by bad theatrical habits and tricks, by the desire to please the public, by incorrect methods of approach to creativeness, day after day, at every repeated performance (458–460)!

Fully aware of his shortcomings, Stanislavsky was depressed and disappointed, both in himself and the Moscow Art Theatre as a group.

While recuperating in Finland after an exhausting tour, Stanislavsky searched for a solution. His deepening sense of malaise was devastating. He took long walks, searching his soul and his notebooks. In *My Life in Art* he describes one moment of enlightened playing which occurred during a performance of a role he had repeated many times.

I understood that to the genius on the stage this condition almost always comes of itself, in all its fullness and richness. Less talented people receive it less often, on Sundays only, so to say. Those who are even less talented receive it even less often, every twelfth holiday, as it were. Mediocrities are visited by it only on very rare occasions, on leap years, on the twenty-ninth of February. Nevertheless, all men of the stage, from the genius to the mediocrity, are able to receive the creative mood, but it is not given them to control it with their own will. They receive it together with inspiration in the form of a heavenly gift....Are there no technical means for the creation of the creative mood, so that inspiration may appear oftener than is its wont (461)?

What he came to realize was that every great actor was surrounded by a kind of aura which audiences sensed and to which they responded in return. It seemed to Stanislavsky that the focus of this creative aura was in the actors' physicalities at moments when their bodies performed "at the call and beck of the inner demands of their wills" (*My Life in Art* 463). These performers were relaxed, focused and completely involved in the theatrical moment. Like children at play, great artists of all kinds could completely concentrate on the task at hand.

The difficulty with this artistic mental condition, what Stanislavsky came to call the "creative mood," lay in summoning this state at will, which seemed nearly impossible. While his recent work had felt forced and shallow, Stanislavsky knew he had experienced this "creative mood" during happier times. In such instances he felt as if fully alive on the stage, radiating with an artistic fire and energy which allowed for total concentration and focus. Stanislavsky realized that this "creative mood" is that "spiritual and physical mood during which it is easiest for inspiration to be born" (*My Life in Art* 462). He believed that:

> If it is impossible to own it at once, then one must put it together bit by bit, using various elements for its construction. If it is necessary to develop each of the component elements in one's self separately, systematically, by a series of certain exercises—let it be so! If the ability to receive the creative mood in its full measure is given to the genius by nature, then perhaps ordinary people may reach a like state after a great deal of hard work with themselves,—not in its full measure, but at least in part (*My Life in Art* 462).

Searching for a method to release this creative power became Stanislavsky's overwhelming task.

Stanislavsky's early search resulted in a number of written accounts, among them the *Draft Manual* begun in Finland in 1906. Between 1906 and 1913 a series of notebooks and other writings emerged. They included the *Reference Book for the Dramatic Actor* and *Practical Information and Good Advice for Beginners and Students of Dramatic Art*, dated 1907, and in the notebooks for 1908 and after were entries on specific topics such as: Introduction, Hackwork, Performance, New Trend (General Foundation), Being [Experiencing], Truth, Logic of Feelings, Emotional Feelings, Roots of Feelings, Will, Muscles, Eradicating Cliches, Objectives, Desires, Communication, Adaptation, Kernel, Through-line of Action, Circles, Tempo, Characterization, Analysis, Self-analysis, How to Use the System, Annotation, Terminology (Stanislavsky Archive Nos. 906–934 qtd. in Benedetti 190).

As early as 1909, Stanislavsky felt prepared to present some of his ideas in public, delivering a paper which introduced what came to be known as the "Magic If." This idea became one of the cornerstones of the "system" and concerns the following question: The actor knows, intellectually, that everything around him is illusory, but IF the circumstances of the play as devised by the author were reality, how would the actor as the character react?

In his notes Stanislavsky listed a six step process:

> 1. The stimulation of the "will," the creation of a commitment to the author's text
> 2. The personal, inner search for psychological material
> 3. "experience" or the process of inner creation in which an actor comes to terms with a character which is not his own and merges with it
> 4. "physicalizing" or the process by which the actor gives the character a bodily image

5. synthesis of the inner and outer, psychological and physical
6. making an impact on the audience (qtd. in Benedetti 190)

Stanislavsky continued in this vein for many years and much of this material eventually was incorporated in the opening sections of *An Actor Prepares*.

While working on the details of the "system" Stanislavsky defined three trends or schools of the actor's art.[1] These he delineated as the school of the proficient or hack actor, the school of representation and the school of lived experience. The first of these three was the old school whereby actors learned by imitation, repeating stock gestures and interpretations handed down from one generation of actors to another.

The second school, that of representation, was identified by Stanislavsky as that of the best in French acting traditions. It consisted of finding emotional truths during the preparatory period, making them external and then reproducing them technically.

What Stanislavsky hoped to create was the third school in which an actor is required to recreate emotions with each performance. He realized that total identification with a character became a pathological condition, but he never fully defined the degree to which an actor must remain detached and maintain control.

Stanislavsky also realized that performance was always a mixture of these three schools and never purely one or another. The defining element was a matter of proportion. Clearly he believed that the school of lived experience must predominate for there to be real theatre. Furthermore, for Stanislavsky, real theatre could only exist if it were free from domination by starring actors or overwhelming authors. Instead, he longed for a theatre built by an ensemble of artists working in concert toward a common goal.

In the years which followed his crisis in Finland, Stanislavsky drew to himself those few colleagues and disciples who shared his vision, hopes and dreams concerning the possibilities for a renewed theatre and a reborn actor. Among them were Evgenii Vakhtangov, Mikhail Chekhov and Richard Boleslavsky, all of whom would make immeasurable contributions, not only to the studios of the Moscow Art Theatre but to all of western theatre practice. As important as these three men were to the project, however, their work would have been fruitless without the guidance, collaboration and boundless energy of Leopold Sulerzhitskii.

Sulerzhitskii appeared to be the only person who, in 1906, recongnized the significance of Stanislavsky's discoveries in Finland. A colorful adventurer and gifted storyteller, Sulerzhitskii was well known and loved by the members of the Moscow Art Theatre. A theatre non-professional and well versed in Eastern philosophy and mysticism,

Sulerzhitskii embraced Stanislavsky's views about the necessity of unearthing the actor's creative potential from the recesses of the mind.

Sulerzhitskii also saw that the first step toward awakening the creative mood was the development of both physical and psychophysical exercises. His enthusiasm for the new ideas made Sulerzhitskii a constant companion for Stanislavsky, who then created an official position for Sulerzhitskii, that of Stanislavsky's first assistant. Together they set out to find the pathway which would allow a deeper communication between actor and audience, something especially required by the new Symbolist dramas which had been so problematic for the Povarskaya Studio. This search, begun in 1906, would eventually lead to the founding of the First Studio of the Moscow Art Theatre in 1912.

"Suler," as Sulerzhitskii was known by his friends and colleagues, is remembered by many as the "soul" of the First Studio. In his memoirs, A. D. Popov characterizes the indomitable Suler in the following fashion:

> The soul of the studio appeared in L. A. Sulerzhitskii. The circle of this man's duties was very hard to define. He was not only a director of the studio, but also a "class mentor," an administrator and electrician (if the lights failed,) also as author of unending numbers of scenarios for exercises and improvisations as well as the creator of posters, if it was necessary to hang up such posters in the studio (91).[2]

Indeed, Leopold Sulerzhitskii was completely devoted to, as well as absolutely necessary to, the operation of the First Studio.

As Stanislavsky's assistant, Suler had been involved with several productions at the Moscow Art Theatre, among them *The Bluebird* by Maeterlinck in 1908 and Shakespeare's *Hamlet* directed by Gordon Craig in 1911. To every production on which he worked Suler contributed his wide range of talents, further enhanced by a tremendous zest for life and an unfailing regard for all of humanity.

In his youth, Suler had studied painting and was quite an accomplished artist. His eye for image and composition was an important element in his work as a director. He also displayed a great talent for music, playing many different instruments. Perhaps his greatest talent, however, was his ability to work with young people, drawing from them the very best they had to offer.

The Studio members were able to relax in Suler's presence in a way they could not when working with Stanislavsky, who could be rather intimidating. The relationship between the actors and Suler was both friendly and mutually respectful and helped to create an atmosphere in which the young people were not afraid to pursue their own creative ideas. Suler could support the actors' personal quests while gently guiding them, both directly and by example. Polyakova explains Suler's charm in the following way:

> Stanislavsky was loved, respected, depended upon, set apart from the mundane by the "aura of genius" which he alone, evidently, was unaware of. Suler was "one of the boys" to everyone he met, be they peasants, soldiers, sailors and fishermen or intellectuals like the Art people. At his ease with everyone, he was delightfully easy to be with—an inexhaustible fount of humour, unboundedly observant and infinitely kind (184).

It was this talent for friendship which Suler displayed that facilitated his relationship with the young Studio members.

Young people also responded well to Suler's enjoyment of "life in all its guises" (Polyakova 184). Suler traveled widely, especially during his youth when he worked as a sailor. He spent time in exile, after being deemed an "unreliable element" and later was a regular guest of Lev Tolstoy at his estate in Yasnaya Polyana, near the town of Tula. Suler was a strong believer in Tolstoy's teachings on moral self-perfection and freely shared those beliefs with his students. He also spent some time in the Canadian wilderness, sent there at Tolstoy's request to help the Dukhobors settle in their adopted homeland.[3] Suler had fallen in love with the theatre as a child and throughout his life displayed many different artistic talents, yet, according to Polyakova, he might not have settled so completely into a life in the theatre had he not become so closely associated with, and indispensable to, Stanislavsky (185). The close relationship between Stanislavsky and Suler remained strong and lasted until Suler's death in 1916.

While the Studio on Povarskaya had been devoted to finding new theatrical forms, by 1912 Stanislavsky felt certain that more important than a new form was the need for new actors. In his first attempts to find a new way of acting, he held workshop rehearsals with the Moscow Art Theatre actors. Most of these performers had been working for many years as professionals and they found the return to a classroom situation very trying. Many were skeptical about Stanislavsky's "system" and believed that if it were all he claimed it to be, he would be a better actor himself. They resented his efforts to return them, established professionals, to their "theatrical ABC's," a process which was known to reduce such veterans as Knipper-Chekhova and even Lilina, Stanislavsky's own wife, to tears (Polyakova 213). His colleagues took little comfort in the knowledge that Stanislavsky always placed himself under the microscope first.

Since the crisis in 1906 Konstantin Sergeevich had lost his enthusiasm for his own performances and they continued to suffer as a result. He believed, nevertheless, that he and Suler could codify his years of acting work into a form that could be of use to other actors. He therefore planned a school which would offer "comprehensive training in the art of experiencing—living—a role." This was remarkable for its time, since none of the many theatre schools worldwide had adopted such a goal (Polyakova 215).

Stanislavsky organized what would be known as the First Studio as a laboratory in which to experiment with his ideas concerning actor training. His attempts between 1906 and 1912 to work with experienced actors had convinced Stanislavsky of the necessity to find fresh, relatively inexperienced actors for his studio. He did not, however, seek "raw beginners." Instead, he wanted to "form young actors who had sufficient experience of professional theatre to recognize their difficulties and know the problems involved but who were not yet fixed in their ways" (Benedetti 198). He began to look for members among the students of the several Moscow acting schools, as well as among the most recently accepted new members of the Moscow Art Theatre company.

It was natural that Stanislavsky would involve Suler in the organization and administration of this new studio. Sulerzhitskii had worked closely with Stanislavsky since 1906, serving as his personal assistant and paid, not by the Moscow Art Theatre, but out of Stanislavsky's own pocket. Suler had been involved since 1907 in the formulation of the beginning exercises and had occasionally taught classes at the Moscow Art Theatre as well as at various theatre schools. His classes in relaxation techniques, breath control, bodily tension and mental concentration offered the first contact between Stanislavsky's ideas and the young actors who wanted to learn them. In reality, while the Studio was considered a branch of the Moscow Art Theatre and was devoted to Stanislavsky and the development of his actor training program, the actual daily operation fell almost entirely to Suler during the first stage of the Studio's existence.

The Moscow Art Theatre had for many years operated a school to train new members. Due to lack of space, however, only a very few out of the hundreds of applicants could be accepted. Many of the disappointed hopefuls then entered one of several private drama schools in Moscow, such as Adashev's school, where Suler and several members of the Art Theatre taught classes.

Many of this younger generation of actors sought more opportunity for public performance than they found at any school. Although they occasionally appeared in roles at the Art Theatre, their stage experience was usually limited to crowd scenes in such favorites of the standard repertoire as *Tsar Fyodor Ivanovich* or *The Living Corpse (Живой труп.)* Of course, these young actors had all been coached by

Stanislavsky and Suler to believe implicitly in their characters, no matter how small the role, and all were eager to test in full-length plays what had gradually become known as "the Stanislavsky system." Indeed, many rehearsals for the fledgling actors had been conducted as lessons in the "system." These eager young people became the core members of the new Studio.

As mentioned above, Sulerzhitskii was the natural choice to head the Studio. Having worked closely with Stanislavsky since 1906, he possessed a subtle grasp of the "system" and "was better able to explain it in practical terms than was its originator himself" (Polyakova 216). In addition to class with Suler were classes held by Evgenii Vakhtangov.

Vakhtangov had been a student in the Adashev school for a year when, in 1910, he was brought by Suler to meet Stanislavsky and Nemirovich-Danchenko. They were very impressed with the young man and eventually he became a member of the Moscow Art Theatre.[4] Stanislavsky soon came to believe that the new member could one day be a great teacher.

In August of 1911, when Stanislavsky wanted to begin classes in the "system," he originally gave control to Vakhtangov, telling him that he should do his best to help those of his colleagues who wanted to learn and if the administrators of the theatre should question him, he should pass the buck back to Stanislavsky himself. Vakhtangov agreed to the plan and several young members of the theatre were invited to attend informal classes.

Lessons were held in the apartment of B. M. Afonin, an actor of the Moscow Art Theatre. The students worked on focus, relaxation, and their inner naïveté. Among these first students were L. E. Deikun, S. G. Birman, S. V. Giatsintova and B. M. Afonin. These lessons were quietly and unofficially supervised by Suler. In the spring of 1912 the students gave a demonstration of their work and plans were made to continue in the fall (Khersonsky 79–81).

While Suler operated the Studio under the overall supervision of Stanislavsky, there was never any indication of conflict or competition between them. Fortunately, these two creative geniuses had the ability to work remarkably well together, creating a partnership which was strong and effective. Polyakova characterizes it as follows:

> Suler combined two normally incongruous qualities—he was a perfectly deferential aide, possessed of an almost telepathic understanding of what Stanislavsky wanted and a remarkable ability to convey it to the young actors; simultaneously, however, he was no truckling nonentity but had a powerful and independent creative personality (216).

It was this powerful creative personality which drew the young people to Suler and made them completely devoted to him.

Many of the young people were also attracted to Suler's Tolstoian philosophies. Stanislavsky summarized Suler's love of the studio as an outgrowth of his philosophy as follows:

> Why did he love the Studio so much? Because it fulfilled one of his greatest life goals: to bring together people with each other, create a common cause, common goals, common labor and joy, to fight banality, violence and injustice, to serve love and nature, beauty and god (qtd. in Markov 256).[5]

This was a philosophy which appealed to the eager young actors and directors and they responded with wholehearted enthusiasm.

Suler loved his young students and was said to have a young soul himself. He could talk to the students freely and as mentioned above, they did not fear him as they often did Stanislavsky. The members of the studio accepted Suler's authority without question and eagerly awaited his classes, gladly meeting his demands. It was Suler's philosophical bent, however, which also led to much discussion of the nature of studios in general.

There came to be some disagreement over the monastic nature of Suler's style. A studio could easily become almost a sect of believers, locked into a single world view and creative style, limiting individual creativity. A question arose for the Studio: Should the evolution of a studio be limited to a single world view and a single style of work or should a studio overcome its tendency towards exclusivity and join the general circle of life, developing a wider world view, and eventually become a true theatre? For many, this conflict defined a difficult moment in the conversion of "studio" into "theatre."

While Suler's personal philosophical agendas tended toward the monastic, he was actually an open-minded seeker who was always eager to experiment with new ideas in his quest for answers in life and art. One outgrowth of his search was his annual trek, accompanied by many Studio members, to the Studio property near Yevpatoria in the Crimea. Here the members lived close to nature, pursuing activities dear to the heart of Suler the Tolstoian. Here, as in all of his work, Suler was a teacher, not only of art, but also of life.

Not only were Konstantin Sergeevich and Suler interested in developing the "system," with their studio they hoped to create "a spiritual order of actors" (*My Life in Art* 537). They envisioned a "temple" of dramatic art which would offer a total experience to the audience. They dreamed of acquiring an estate connected by streetcar line or railroad to a major city. There the actors would live and guests would come to occupy a room for the night and enjoy an evening of theatre. The finances for such a venture were to come, not only from the performances, but from cottage industry and agricultural cultivation of the soil, to be done by the actors.

In pursuit of this goal, Stanislavsky purchased the large plot of land in the Crimea which he presented to the Studio in 1912. During the summers which followed, communal buildings, a small hotel, a stable, a cow shed, barns and an ice house were built. Each actor was to build his own house with his own labor. This house would then become the actor's property.

During the summers of 1913–1916 a group of the Studio actors went to Yevpatoria with Sulerzhitskii and attempted to realize the dream. While the vision of Stanislavsky and Suler was never fully realized, it did serve to bring the members of the studio closer together, outside of the "close and nervous atmosphere of the stage" (*My Life in Art* 537– 539).

The results of living and working so closely together became evident when the studio began to perform for an audience. As Markov recalls,

> This could not fail to be communicated to the spectators, when they saw the performances of the actors grouped around this strange and inspired person. That was why what was necessary was the form of a studio—a form of fraternal co-operation and close, self-contained intimacy—in order more completely and with greater concentration to communicate to the audience that which Sulerzhitskii bore within himself and which he aroused in the feelings of those with whom he worked. He aspired in the theatre toward what was most true and truthful and for this reason he often seemed to sin against theatricality (255).[6]

These sins, in Markov's view, might have remained unredeemed if not for the work of Suler's student and follower, Evgenii Vakhtangov. Whatever his failings may have been, Suler, nevertheless, always demanded from his students that which he gave himself: the deepest commitment to aesthetics, ethics and creativity.

It was this commitment to ethics, closely bound to his sense of aesthetics and creativity, which caused Suler to view training in the "system" as a means toward training not only actors but people in general. He believed that the "system" could deepen a person's view of life and allow him or her to live free from skepticism and with the joy of living which he, Suler, possessed (Markov 255–258).

Suler knew, however, the dangers inherent in improper use of the "system." He saw instances when work on the inner actor led toward hysteria and away from truth, a condition against which he often wrote. He believed that hysterical acting showed, not a depth of experiencing the role, but an illness of the nerves which then could lead to "rubber stamp" performances. For Suler, it was of utmost importance that every speech given by an actor on the stage be a new creation born of living the role, not simply the result of hysteria spreading from one actor and infecting all the others (Markov 261–263).

Suler saw the move away from hysteria towards truth and purity in performance as a question of both aesthetics and ethics. As a result, it was in the nature of the studio to search for both ethics in art and art in ethics (Markov 264). This search continued in one form or another for many years.

Stanislavsky knew that it was essential for the Studio to have its own home, separate from the facilities of the Moscow Art Theatre. There is some confusion over the exact location of the Studio's modest facilities. In *My Life in Art* Stanislavsky states, "The hired home of the new Studio was located in the same place where the Society of Art and Literature was first founded, in the same place that once housed the Hunting Club" (531). Other sources indicate that the studio was located in a room above a cinema, The Cinematograph, later known as The Lux (Benedetti 199, Polyakova 217). The question of location is further confused by the fact that Stanislavsky also says, in *My Life in Art*, that the headquarters of the Hunting Club burned down during the time the Society of Art and Literature was housed there and that their performances were stopped while they waited for the new facility to be built. This fire predated the founding of the Moscow Art Theatre and therefore also the Studio by many years.

Whatever may have been the exact location, the sources do agree on the general nature of the facility. The auditorium was very small, in itself an innovative feature. Polyakova writes, "The stage and the few rows of unadorned seats were on the same level," (218) while Benedetti contends that only the front row was on the stage level and that the auditorium floor was raked (199). Both agree that space was very limited, seating, perhaps, only fifty people.

The result of this tiny performance space was an increased feeling of intimacy between the actors and audience. The slightest gesture or the most subtle change of expression could be clearly seen from the back of the house. In the absence of the "fourth wall" of the proscenium arch, the stage and auditorium merged and empathy came to border on a state of symbiosis, in which the audience identified with the characters no less intimately than did the actors themselves (Polyakova 218).

The nature of the facility, in combination with the limitations of funding, supported the emphasis on acting technique as opposed to spectacle in Studio productions. In fact, spectacle was nearly non-existent in the Studio. Old green curtains taken from the Art-Popular theatre were used to separate the acting area from the rows of seats.

Actors easily and often walked across the dividing line to come close to the first rows of the audience.

The small, shallow stage area made complicated or multiple sets impossible. Stage settings were very simple, often consisting of painted backgrounds and minimal furnishings. While the style of the Studio performances was, on the surface, naturalistic, it was in reality much more abstract aesthetically. A painted cloth set gave the sense, not the reality of a room. Often any items of set decoration, if they did not have to be physically handled or manipulated by the actors, were painted onto the set. Clearly, the Studio was not a place for fully mounted public productions, but always a place to work, and that work focused on the actor's craft, both as an individual and as part of the total ensemble of the stage.

The primary tasks of the Studio work were formulated in the following way:

> 1. cultivation of the psychology of the actor's creativity
> 2. elaborating the way the actor feels physically
> 3. bringing the actor closer to the author
>
> The truth of the actor's performance was underlined by the arrangement of a
> stage without footlights or a platform, dictated by external necessity but at the
> same time organic (Markov 270).[7]

At first the studio focused its attention entirely on pedagogy and the training of actors, limiting the work to scenic improvisations, études and excerpts from larger pieces. Then, on January 15, 1913, the Studio presented its first public performance, *The Wreck of the Ship "Hope"* (*Op Hoop Van Zegen*) by the Dutch playwright, Herman Heijermans. This tragedy, which contrasts the downtrodden crew of an unseaworthy ship and the wealthy shipowners who send it to sea in the hope of collecting an insurance claim, was first proposed for the Studio by Richard Boleslavsky. Boleslavsky was a young actor of the Studio who wanted to become a director. He received permission from the administrators to prepare the play with those students who were available and interested.

Work on this production progressed with the assistance of Suler. Boleslavsky would rehearse the actors for a time and then Suler would come in and re-work what had been done. In this way Boleslavsky learned about directing with Suler and, occasionally, Stanislavsky himself acting as a safety net. It was a grueling period for all involved, with rehearsals often taking place at midnight or 2:00 a.m., when other duties were finished.

The Wreck of the Ship "Hope" was a piece which gratified the Tolstoian tendencies in Suler. The heroes of the play were simple, hard working fishermen at the mercy of wealthy, uncaring businessmen. It was also an opportunity for Boleslavsky to expand his understanding of the "system" and contribute to its formulation. Rehearsals included improvisations, "Affective Memory" work and exercises devised by Bolesavsky to embody the rhythm and overall atmosphere of the sea. This early work formed the foundation of Boleslavsky's mastery of the tenets of the "system" which he brought to the United States in 1919. Then, in 1923, Boleslavsky, along with Maria Ouspenskaya, founded the American Theatre Laboratory where classes in the "system" were offered.

The Wreck of the Ship "Hope" was well received by its Moscow audience. It was praised for the clarity of the performances and the ensemble orientation of the troupe, and "critics and audiences were impressed by the unaffected veracity of this maiden effort" (Polyakova 218). While it was a popular piece, it did not, however, have much depth of thought. Boleslavsky had been attracted to the strong emotions portrayed by the playwright. The piece lent itself to a heroic, monumental production but was, of necessity, given in a primitive, studio style.

It was in this minimal production style that the actors took the first steps away from Naturalism toward the "Realism of the Soul" that Suler and Stanislavsky were seeking (Khersonsky 92–93). The production, though flawed, was successful enough that the administrative board of the Moscow Art Theatre agreed to fund the further work of the Studio which had been, up to this time, financed entirely by Stanislavsky personally (*My Life in Art* 531–532).

Buoyed by the reception of their first production, the Studio members embarked on their second piece. It was a dark play by Hauptman, *Holiday of Peace (Das Friedensfest)*. This time the director was Evgenii Vakhtangov, the young man who had held acting classes the previous year for the newly formed Studio. Vakhtangov was familiar with the play, having staged it in 1904 with the amateur actors of the Vladikavaz Students' Workshop in Grozny. He had, at that time, also played the role of Wilhelm. Vakhtangov was eager to attempt the play again, this time with better actors and more rehearsal time (Khersonsky 93).

Holiday of Peace was reminiscent of Ibsen's *Ghosts* in that it dealt with the issues of hereditary illness and the modern moral problems of the bourgeoisie. The characters were egotistical, hysterical people without the strength to live a socially constructive life. They lived in a home without peace, and the family was destroyed. For Vakhtangov, these characters represented, not just one unfortunate family, but all of bourgeois society (Khersonsky 94–95).

When the production was shown on October 15, 1915, there was a less than favorable response. Stanislavsky had seen a dress rehearsal before the opening and was not pleased with what he saw as hysteria which emanated from the actors and infected the audience. Suler, however, urged that the production be shown to invited members of the Moscow Art Theatre.

The reaction of the invited audience was mixed. Unlike *The Wreck of the Ship "Hope,"* the play had no admirable characters. On the contrary, these characters, portrayed in the close confines of the small theatre space, "provoked a wave of hysteria in its spectators" (Gordon 45). The actors gave what Markov calls a "sharpened" (*заостренный*) performance to which the audience strongly responded (282). This heightened emotional tension would reappear in Vakhtangov's future work, as both director and as actor.

The production, furthermore, violated Stanislavsky's own feelings concerning social issues presented on stage. Konstantin Sergeevich preferred plays in which a balanced view was presented that allowed the audience members to form their own opinions based on ideas revealed rather than those that overtly forced a single point of view (Benedetti 223).

Benedetti further describes Stanislavsky's furious response to the rehearsal he witnessed and reports that Konstantin Sergeevich threatened to cancel the show. He also states that Suler and Nemirovich agreed but that it was Kachalov who intervened and convinced the others to allow the performance to go forward. Regardless of who supported whom, the result was the same. The production opened to mixed reviews and an artistic rift opened between Stanislavsky and his favorite student, Vakhtangov, "that was never fully resolved, although personal relations continued affectionate and they engaged in regular argument" (Benedetti 223).

In contrast to the uproar over *Holiday of Peace*, the Studios next production was widely praised and became a cornerstone of the repertoire. During the summer of 1914, the members of the Studio worked on an adaptation of *The Cricket on the Hearth* by Charles Dickens. In opposition to the Hauptmann play, *Cricket* was a celebration of humanity and the human spirit. The emotional impact of the piece was enhanced by its anti-war slant which made a great impression as war fever spread across Russia on the eve of World War I.

The promoter, adapter and director for the piece was B. M. Sushkevich, but the soul of the production was Suler, the Tolstoian humanist. Under his guidance, the play became a spiritual crusade and an attempt to arouse in people the thoughts and feelings which would make war impossible (Khersonsky 114). While Vakhtangov did not disagree with the over-all vision of the production, he did, however, approach his own role differently than did his colleagues.

For the other actors in *Cricket on the Hearth*, the characters were generally noble heroes to be lovingly and sympathetically portrayed. For Vakhtangov, the role of Takleton offered a different challenge. This character was the villain in the piece and Vakhtangov played him with a cold and unforgiving edge. Audiences were enthralled with his portrayal, which grew out of his own poor relationship with his businessman father (Khersonsky 117). Zorgraf characterizes Vakhtangov's approach to *Cricket on the Hearth* in the following way:

> In *Cricket on the Hearth* there are no unaffected and complete personalities, no idealization of the past, no reconciliation of man with reality. In his (Vakhtangov's) performances of it, there unfolded the life of a suffering and condemned man, crippled by a capitalistic city. What interests Vakhtangov is not an idealization of the past, but a merciless exposure of contemporaneity (17).[8]

Vakhtangov's interpretation of his role offered a striking contrast to all the others in the play which, in this instance, enhanced the production as a whole.

In this piece the Studio presented its own vision of Dickensian England, a "toy" England which reflected the benevolent world view that informs the play. The setting presented the modest home of John Periwinkle and his family with warmth and humor. A prologue was written to help set the tone of the play. It explained the cricket singing his songs and the teapot with whom he chats. Then the curtains opened to reveal the poor but comfortable room dominated by the great fireplace.

What followed was a lovely Christmas story of family solidarity in the face of difficulty and the power of love to overcome greed and the evil men sometimes do. While the heroes were played with touching sincerity, Vakhtangov's interpretation of Takleton included a touch of caricature for contrast.

Cricket on the Hearth was a tremendous success and came to epitomize all that was positive in the early years of the Studio under the guidance of Sulerzhitskii. It also marked a change in the status of the Studio in relation to the Moscow Art Theatre. The success of the Studio aggravated the already strained relationship between Stanislavsky and Nemirovich-Danchenko. Nemirovich had urged Stanislavsky for years to drop the idea of the studios because he felt they were unnecessary and took too much time and energy away from the Moscow Art Theatre. There was also some feeling that the Studio would siphon away the best talent from Moscow Art.[9]

With the success of *Cricket on the Hearth* in the fall of 1914, the Studio moved to larger facilities on Skobelevsky Square.[10] During the following year it became clear that Nemirovich was very unhappy with the success of the Studio and wanted it to be reorganized as a separate entity. According to Benedetti, the hidden agenda was to use this reorganization to force Stanislavsky out of the Studio and back to the Moscow Art itself (223).

Since 1911, Stanislavsky had refused to continue carrying out administrative duties in the Moscow Art Theatre. This fact was not, however, generally known since Stanislavsky had not stopped working at the theatre in his other capacities. As the company began to slip in the public's estimation, Stanislavsky felt a need to publicly separate himself from the Moscow Art and devote himself full time to the Studio.

Konstantin Sergeevich also proposed the creation of an international studio which would bring artists from around the world to study the "system." Before this could happen, however, the February revolution of 1917 brought the project to a swift and abrupt halt. The social and political turmoil caused by the revolution impacted many aspects of Stanislavsky's life, but it did not dampen his enthusiasm for his "system" as it was being implemented in the First Studio. In fact, for five years the lessons in the "system" had produced numerous successes, many of which were embodied by the work of one exceptional actor, Mikhail Chekhov.

As Sulerzhitskii, Boleslavsky and Vakhtangov grew in stature as directors at the Studio, so Mikhail Chekhov came to personify the "system" actor's craft. The nephew of the famous writer, Anton Chekhov, this energetic young man gave an impressive audition for Stanislavsky. This audition, in April, 1912, offered a glimpse of the future to Konstantin Sergeevich. Chekhov performed an extract from *Tsar Fyodor* and one of Marmeladov's speeches from Dostoyevsky's *Crime and Punishment*. Chekhov was immediately invited to join the company and become, as Stanislavsky commented to Suler, "One of the real hopes for the future" (Benedetti 199).

During the Moscow Art Theatre's 1912–13 season, Chekhov appeared in small roles in several productions, among them the Gordon Craig *Hamlet* and Moliere's *The Imaginary Invalid*. Then, in 1913, he was cast by Boleslavsky in *The Wreck of the Ship "Hope."* He played a minor role, that of Kobe, an idiot fisherman, which he transformed into a new focus for the play.

Although audiences were thrilled by Chekhov's riveting performance, he was criticized for expanding his role so that it became more than what the playwright had written. This notion that an actor can go beyond the playwright to the true nature of a character was to become the hallmark of Chekhov's work. While he always believed himself to be a disciple of Stanislavsky, sharing many of Konstantin Sergeevich's concerns for the emotional depth of actors' performances, over the years Chekhov would modify the "system" into his own technique, which he then shared with his students, first in Russia then in Europe, England and eventually the United States.

Mikhail Chekhov was an extremely intuitive performer who often improvised around a text, tapping into the natural naïveté and spontaneity Stanislavsky sought to touch with his "system." Chekhov also had the ability to bring out the best in his partners. Many of the actors who worked with him commented that with Chekhov it was not necessary to act but only to react. Certainly his tendency to improvise made it absolutely necessary for his partners to be completely present in the moment, since they could never be sure what he would do.

In Vakhtangov's production of the *Holiday of Peace* Chekhov played Fribe, the alcoholic member of the family. He built his portrayal around the idea that Fribe was aware that each part of his body was slowly dying a separate death. This was contrary to other, standard interpretations of alcoholism and was startlingly impressive to his audience (Gordon 121).

Chekhov's contributions to *Cricket on the Hearth* were instrumental to the success of the production and, ultimately, the Studio itself. He played the role of Caleb the toymaker and in preparation for the role Chekhov built all the mechanical toys for the production. In this way he became closely acquainted with the soul of his character, which he then translated into the physical embodiment of the old man. This performance offered a strong contrast to Vakhtangov's Takelton and gave equilibrium to the production of *Cricket* as a whole.

The next important production of the First Studio was Berger's *The Flood,* directed by Vakhtangov. This piece, set in a bar in an American town, premiered on December 14, 1915. The play dramatized a striking psychological contrast, while the production itself came to symbolize the basic conflict within the Studio at that time. The play centers around a group of unsavory characters who are assembled in a bar when they learn of an approaching flood which threatens their lives. During the course of the three acts the playwright contrasts two different aspects of the characters: the way they behave under normal conditions and the way they behave when their lives are threatened.

For Vakhtangov, the three act construction offered a structural mirror of the theme. That is, in the first act, the characters behave "like wolves" towards each other. Then in the second act, when their lives are in danger, they come to penitence and confession. Finally, in the third act when the danger has passed and all are safe, they return to all the disagreeable behavioral patterns they had displayed in the first act (Markov 282).

Vakhtangov interpreted the play as a denunciation of bourgeois society. The characters in it are hard, mercenary and more interested in money than in humanity. The fact that they return to their former selves once the danger has passed was, for Vakhtangov, proof that bourgeois society deprives people of their higher human instincts. Suler, however, saw the play differently which caused considerable friction between the two men. Suler believed in the basic goodness of people and felt that this play about horrid people opening their hearts to one another would also open the hearts of the audience. He anticipated that the performance would evoke a sort of "Christian catharsis" (Khersonsky 118–120). This interpretation coincided with Suler's view of the earlier production, *The Wreck of the Ship "Hope."* During rehearsals for *"Hope"* Suler told the actors that the poetry of disaster unites people. He believed that people came together in a disaster, not to talk about trouble but to be close, to search together, to support one another and commiserate. This was the approach he took to both *"Hope"* and *Flood*.

Vakhtangov, for his part, found it very difficult to rehearse the second act. Time and again he would break off rehearsal at the same point because he detected only falseness in the performers. To him, the sincerity the actors tried to convey was totally unconvincing. Finally, in desperation, he sat down at the piano and began to play out his frustration. Without any plan, the actors began to hum along, wordlessly. Through this means, Vakhtangov and the actors found the inner truth of the characters and brought the scene to life. Khersonsky describes the moment as follows:

> Thus the famous song in "The Flood" was born and the key to the scene of bonding was finally found. Not through thoughts about love and good, not through words about repentance and reconciliation, but through the subconscious, half-animal, half-human mooing of people, who have huddled together from their horror of death. Faster, louder!... Now more joyfully already. Having felt themselves together, they are no longer so afraid. There is communicated to them each other's warmth and rhythm, they are caught up by the physiological sensation of life and mutual support (121).[11]

Once this key to the scene was found by happy accident, Vakhtangov was able to use this moment as a gesture of protest against Sulers more benevolent outlook and make more pointed the contrast with the acts which preceded and followed, thus advancing his own interpretation of the play.

Unfortunately, the conflict with Suler, who was supported by Stanislavsky, caused the performances to waiver somewhere between the pointed satire Vakhtangov wanted and the hopeful humanism of Suler. Vakhtangov was unhappy about the interference of the two administrators who overruled his work and he soon lost his enthusiasm for the piece (Khersonsky 122).

Another conflict in the production of *The Flood* involved acting styles. Vakhtangov had double cast himself and Mikhail Chekhov in the role of Fraser, a bankrupt merchant. Chekhov interpreted the role with a humor approaching farce, while Vakhtangov's much more subdued and serious portrayal leaned toward tragi-comedy. In this instance it was the audiences who determined the outcome, since they clearly preferred Chekhov's portrayal to Vakhtangov's. Finally Vakhtangov began to imitate Chekhov's interpretation of the role, as did other actors who followed him.

One year after the production of *The Flood*, disaster struck the First Studio. On December 17, 1916 Leopold Sulerzhitskii died of chronic nephritis. His death and the resultant confusion and floundering of the Studio corresponded to the approaching upheaval in Russian society. It was a difficult time both inside and outside the Studio and it marked the end of an era.

With the death of Suler, the leadership of the Studio fell to Vakhtangov for a time. The notable productions of the period reflect the changes in attitude that followed the change of leadership. Lighthearted and hopeful plays like *Cricket on the Hearth* made way for darker, more pessimistic productions such as Ibsen's *Rosmersholm* in 1918 and Strindberg's *Erik XIV* in 1921. In his staging of these pieces Vakhtangov began to find his own style, often providing graphic contrasts on the stage. For example, the concept behind the visual aspects of *Rosmersholm* was the use of light to emphasize the psychology of the characters. By focusing light on the hands and faces of the actors, Vakhtangov drew the audience's attention to the people and away from their surroundings.

In *Erik XIV* the goal was the graphic depiction of two worlds, of the living and of the dead. In this production, the members of the royal court were played as if they were dead, bloodless and cold, while the simple villagers were warm, loving and full of life.

The role of Erik, assigned to Mikhail Chekhov, presented him with a challenge that would allow him to realize one of his finest achievements as an actor. He struggled to find an interpretation that would balance the contradictions in this tortured character. What Chekhov attempted to portray was the conflict within the king who glimpses a better life away from the throne but is compelled to remain king. Chekhov devised for himself an image which helped him discover the inner nature of the character; the image of Erik trapped inside a circle. The socially impotent king attempts to touch something of life but his hands do not make contact. In this instance Chekhov moved away from Stanislavsky's emphasis on "Affective Memory" and used an external image and physicality to create a striking performance (Gordon 127).

It is interesting to note that Chekhov was at that time simultaneously preparing two of his greatest roles, that of Erik at the Studio and Khlestakov in Gogol's *Inspector General (Ревизор)* at the Moscow Art Theatre. These plays and their characters were as unlike each other as possible, yet Chekhov stunned his colleagues and his audiences with his complete mastery of each.

By the autumn of 1921 there was a great deal of disorder and dissatisfaction in the Studio. During the years of revolution and civil war, many things happened to complicate the relationship between the Studios and the Moscow Art Theatre. Primary among them was the situation that developed when most of the leading members of the Moscow Art Theatre, on tour in Kharkov, found themselves on the wrong side of the battle lines, unable, and in some cases unwilling, to return to Moscow. This situation lasted for three years, and eventually some members of the First and Second Studios stepped into roles on the parent stage. The missing actors, under the leadership of Vassily Kachalov, returned in 1922 in order to travel on an extended tour with the Moscow Art Theatre to Europe and America. While the parent company was touring, the Studio members who were left behind continued to operate the Moscow Art.

Another difficulty, which continued for several years, arose following the death of Sulerzhitskii. As previously noted, following Suler's death the leadership of the First Studio fell to Vakhtangov. At this time Vakhtangov was also involved with several other studios, among them his own Mansurovsky Studio, which would eventually become the Third Studio of the Moscow Art Theatre. Vakhtangov's many commitments as director and teacher did not allow him to devote himself as totally to the First Studio as Suler had, and the actors increasingly assumed more responsibility themselves. Then, when Vakhtangov died in 1922, the Studio was again without leadership.

The person who took on the primary responsibility in this area was Mikhail Chekhov. As Chekhov began to take charge of rehearsals, it became evident that he was neither the teacher nor the director that Vakhtangov had been. O. I. Pyzhova relates that when Chekhov would attempt to demonstrate for a colleague, he was more likely to hinder than to help. Chekhov often did not know himself how he did what he did. Furthermore, the actor watching Chekhov play a role often felt too intimidated or inadequate to attempt to copy the master (69–70). These circumstances combined to cause a loss of focus in the Studio as well as a dissatisfaction with the organization of the group. Some members felt the Studio should separate entirely from Moscow Art, while others believed the best thing would be for the Moscow Art Theatre to completely absorb the Studio so that it no longer existed as a separate entity.

In November of 1921 the Board of the First Studio met to discuss whether or not to join with the Art Theatre, but no decision was reached. Vakhtangov urged Stanislavsky to abandon the Art Theatre and start fresh with the Studio. Konstantin Sergeevich was greatly distressed by this turn of events, but "The Studios, his babies, had grown up and wanted their independence, regardless of what their parents might think" (Smeliansky 39). Finally, in 1924, while Stanislavsky was on tour with the Art Theatre in America, Nemirovich-Danchenko formally altered the Studio/Theatre relationship and made the First Studio into the Second Moscow Art Theatre under the leadership of Mikhail Chekhov, a move which infuriated Stanislavsky. In a letter dated June 10, 1924, Stanislavsky refers to the First Studio as, "this long-standing sickness of my soul" which had betrayed the Moscow Art Theatre "in every respect" (*Moscow Art Theatre Letters* 324).[12] Stanislavsky saw himself as King Lear, betrayed by his beloved daughters, his Studios. The First Studio became his Goneril when it became the Second Art Theatre. This Second Art Theatre would be eliminated by Josef Stalin in 1936.

The First Studio of the Moscow Art Theatre served an invaluable function in the world of Western theatre. It was here that what came to be Stanislavsky's "system" was devised and tested. It was also a laboratory for experimentation in both actor training and performance style. During the twelve years of its existence, the First Studio passed through several eras or phases of work, each of which added concepts to the "system" while expanding production practices and techniques. Here the young generation of actors learned from Suler, not only how to be good actors, but how to be good people.

Without the input and impetus of the First Studio, it is possible that the "system" would never have been as well defined as it was. It certainly could not have been tested as thoroughly had Stanislavsky been forced to rely on the half-hearted attempts made by the Moscow Art Theatre members. It was at the Studio that Stanislavsky could finally see his theories in practice. The Studio also provided the opportunity for Stanislavsky's disciples and colleagues to contribute their own ideas and experiences to the process.

The First Studio was the birthplace, not only of the "system" which has so thoroughly dominated Western theatrical training in this century, but also the incubator for the greatest teachers and practitioners of that "system" who then shared their knowledge with others around the world. It was in the First Studio that Evgenii Vakhtangov honed his skills as teacher and director. The contrast between his basically somber view of humanity and Suler's optimism added depth to the landmark works of the Studio. This darker world view then came to dominate the Studio work after the death of Suler and also carried over into Vakhtangov's other projects, which will be discussed at length in Chapter 4.

Boleslavsky and the American Theatre Laboratory, Evgenii Vakhtangov with his landmark productions at his numerous other studios and Mikhail Chekhov, arguably the finest character actor of the century, all grew from roots planted and nourished at the First Studio. And it is from those same roots that a major body of Western theatre practice in this century has grown and flourished.

Scene I, *Wreck of the Ship "Hope"* by H. Heijermans, First Studio 1913

Cricket on the Hearth by Charles Dickens, First Studio 1914

Mikhail Chekhov as Caleb in *Cricket on the Hearth*, First Studio 1914

Evgenii Vakhtangov as Takleton in *Cricket on the Hearth*

Scene from *Flood* by G. Berger, First Studio 1915

Scene from *Flood* by G. Berger, First Studio 1915

Vakhtangov as Fraser in *Flood*

Chekhov as Fraser in *Flood*

S. Birman as the Queen in *Erik XIV*, First Studio 1921

Mikhail Chekhov as Erik in *Erik XIV*

CHAPTER THREE

The Second Studio:
A New Generation Evolves

Beginning almost with the founding of the Moscow Art Theatre, Konstantin Stanislavsky searched for the talented young people he knew would be needed to keep his theatre alive. Both Stanislavsky and Nemirovich-Danchenko were fully aware that, like a living organism, the Moscow Art Theatre would need to replenish itself, finding and nurturing artists who could join the ensemble, bringing new blood and youthful vitality into the company. While there was always, therefore, a training component to the Moscow Art Theatre community, it was not until 1924 that those who would be known as the "Second Generation" would officially become full members of the company. These talented young people came almost entirely from the Second Studio of the Moscow Art Theatre, the only one of the primary studios which came to be completely assimilated within the parent organization.

The official founding of the Second Studio of the Moscow Art Theatre is generally dated as November 24, 1916, the date on which the premiere performance of the Studio's first production took place. Like all of the Moscow Art Theatre's studios, however, its real beginning is not so easily defined. Of course this studio, like all the studios, grew out of Stanislavsky's crisis of 1906; but more specifically, the Second Studio was an outgrowth of the School of Dramatic Art, operated by three artists of the Moscow Art known as the "Three Nikolais": Nikolai Massalitinov, Nikolai Podgorny and Nikolai Aleksandrov.

In the spring of 1916, some students of the School of Dramatic Art or Massalitinov School, as it was also known, were invited to join with some earlier graduates of the school and some promising young aspirants to the Art Theatre in the creation of the new Second Studio of the

Moscow Art Theatre. Among these young actors were A. K. Tarasova, T. I. Duvan, E. I. Kornakova, R. N. Molchanova, L. I. Zueva, M. I. Puzireva, I. Y. Sudakov, A. P. Zueva, V. S. Sokolova, N. P. Batalov, E. V. Kaluzhskii, E. K. Elena, V. A. Verbitskii, V. P. Redlikh, G. P. Udin, V. P. Istrin, M. A. Krizhanovskaya and others. The primary initiator of the project was Vakhtang L. Mchedelov.

Mchedelov was a man of great temperament and energy. His complete devotion to the theatre made it possible for him to overcome many obstacles, including his father's objections to a career in art. In 1904, Mchedelov came to Moscow to enter the philology department of Moscow University. He became enamored of the Moscow Art Theatre and began to train there, moving towards directing rather than pursuing an acting career. In the 1914/15 and 1915/16 seasons he served as an assistant director under Nemirovich-Danchenko on the productions of *Autumn Violins (Осенние скрипки)* by I. Surguchov and *There Will Be Joy (Будет радость)* by D. Merezhkovskii while, at the same time, working as a teacher at the School of Dramatic Art.

When it became known that the school would soon close, Mchedelov decided to independently bring together a group of students to prepare a play by Zinaida Gippius, *The Green Ring (Зеленое кольцо)*[1] with the intention of eventually showing it to Stanislavsky. The ultimate goal was to convince Konstantin Sergeevich to permit these young students to form what they hoped would be the Second Studio.

Rehearsals began in the summer of 1916 and when the young people came together in the autumn the new studio had, in reality, already been formed. Its connection with the Moscow Art was further established when Mchedelov approached three of the company's experienced actors, A. A. Stakhovich, N. N. Litovtseva and I. E. Duvan, with the proposition that they perform the roles of the older characters in the play. The veterans agreed and began rehearsals with Mchedelov. Then, on October 8, 1916, the young director arranged a showing of the second act of *The Green Ring* for Stanislavsky. At this time the first and third acts were also performed for Konstantin Sergeevich, not on the stage but around a table.

This important rehearsal took place in the first facilities of the Studio. Mchedelov had located for his group a small building on Milyutinskii Lane with a large room on the second floor. Here, in a hall which could hold no more than one hundred people, the young men and women set to work on their project. Ivanova describes the momentous occasion when the young hopefuls first met with the master. "The actors—young men, girls seventeen to nineteen years old, for the first time met with the head of the Art theater....So. He, Stanislavsky, in this small space, surrounded by young, embarrassed faces. A crowd of teenagers waits for him to decide their fate" (103).[2] To their great relief, his reaction was favorable and they continued to rehearse the play.

It was particularly appropriate, at that time, for the young people to prepare this production, since it was one of several contemporary plays which attempted to answer the questions of the new generation. *The Green Ring* tells the story of a group of high-school students, searching for their places in the world during a time of uncertainty. In 1916 the future was far from settled and young people all over Russia were searching for their own places in the new order which was coming. The young artists and actors related strongly to the characters in Gippius' play who were also struggling with the philosophies of work and the problems of life.

For Stanislavsky the performances of the young people, while quite promising, lacked a spark which he hoped to find and develop. He spent many hours simply talking with the actors, searching for a youthful joyfulness and love of life. Stanislavsky hoped to build a psychological base for the actors by exploring their own youthful outlooks (Ivanova 104).

It was decided that rehearsals should continue and that the piece would be shown to the Art Theatre community in November, before opening for the public. The general rehearsal, held on November 24, 1916, was a tremendous success. While the critics generally held that the play was flawed and pretentious, the young actors themselves were highly praised. Since Nemirovich-Danchenko was also quite pleased with the production, the new Studio was off to a strong start and *The Green Ring* remained in the repertoire until 1924.

The story of *The Green Ring* centers around a young girl, Finochka, and her circle of friends, the "Green Ring." Alla Tarasova, in the role of Finochka, was particularly praised by the critics for her performance. Her beautiful voice and large, shining eyes led reviewers to compare her favorably with Vera Komissarzhevskaya, the popular St. Petersburg actress who had just died in 1910 at the age of forty-six. At this time Tarasova was only eighteen years old, but many in the auditorium believed they were witnessing the premier performance of a woman who would become one of the leading actresses of the Russian stage, a belief that was later to be confirmed.

The premiere of *The Green Ring* was a momentous occasion for both the Studio and the Moscow Art Theatre. Following its great success, many of the Art Theatre actors became involved with training the young Studio members. Among those who served as teachers were L. M. Leonidov, V. V. Luzhskii, N. N. Litovtseva, N. A. Podgornii, N. O. Massalitinov and N. A. Alexandrov. Occasionally Stanislavsky himself entered into the work, as did Vakhtangov.

As the Second Studio approached its second season, momentous events were rocking Russia. In February and then October of 1917 Russia was torn by revolution.[3] The first revolt overthrew the tsarist regime and replaced it with a provisional government headed by Kerensky. The second brought the Bolshevik branch of the Communist Party to power and ended Russian involvement in World War I. What followed was a bloody civil war which lasted until 1921.

The social and political changes which accompanied these revolutions and wars influenced all Russians, including theatre artists. For the theatre community, this turbulent time was shaped by the burning question each theatre tried to answer for itself: what role should the theatre play in a socialist society?

Lunacharsky, the first People's Commissar for Education, defined the new order's need for theatre in the following terms:

> The Revolution said to the theatre: "Theatre, I need you. I need you, but not so that I, the Revolution, can relax in comfortable seats in a beautiful hall and enjoy a show after all the hard work and battles....I need you as a helper, as a searchlight, as an advisor. I want to see my friends and enemies on your stage....I want to see them with my own eyes. I want also to study them through your methods" (qtd. in Rudnitsky *Russian and Soviet Theater* 41).

This need for theatre was intensified by the fact that, at the time of the Revolution, eighty percent of the Russian population was illiterate. The new leaders clearly saw that the theatre could serve as both a school and a newspaper for the uneducated masses. Theatre could communicate in a language clearly understood by all Russians. The theatre served as a beacon for millions of workers, peasants and soldiers as they searched for truth in matters of life and death, finding answers to complex political conflicts in performances which often reached incredible levels of excitement and agitation.

For theatre artists it was a time of excitement, but also a time of confusion and searching, as well as a time of financial strain, which lasted until long after the end of the Civil War. Political beliefs were mixed and often not yet well formulated on both the individual and organizational levels. Differences of opinion were frequent and were often strongly expressed, whether between artist and artist or between artist and audience. The entire artistic intelligentsia in general, theatre practitioners included, did not formulate their attitudes towards the new Bolshevik leadership quickly or without hesitation (*Russian and Soviet Theater* 41).

During the second season of the Studio the students prepared a production titled *Studio Diary* (*Дневник студии*) which was a compilation of three adaptations: *No Way Out* (*Некуда*) taken from a novel by N. S. Leskov, three pieces taken from *The Story of Lieutenant Ergunov* (*История лейтенанта Ергунова*) by Turgenev and an adaptation taken from *White Nights* (*Белыу ночи*) by Dostoyevsky. During the early years of the Revolution, performances such as this which were taken from classics of Russian literature were very popular. The new Russian audience was excited by the opportunity to enjoy works which had previously been reserved for the social elite. Performances of the classics, furthermore, opened a door for uncompromising criticism of the former feudal, bourgeois and bureaucratic system. Class privilege could be ridiculed and the most sympathetic heroes were those who championed the rights of the common folk (*Russian and Soviet Theater* 48).

Studio Diary was directed by Nikolai Massalitinov and E. F. Krasnopolskaya and was first shown to an audience on February 14, 1918. The play was so successful it was re-worked, re-arranged and reinstated into the repertoire several times between 1918 and 1928.

Originally *Studio Diary* was not expected to be more than an educational exercise for the Studio members, but eventually a part of *No Way Out* and all of *The Story of Lieutenant Ergunov* entered the studio repertoire. Beginning in the 1918/19 season, *Lieutenant Ergunov* was presented together with scenes adapted from the novel *Decembrists* (*Декабристы*) by Merezhkovskii and one chapter of *The Brothers Karamazov* (*Братья Карамазовы*) by Dostoyevsky.

During its first years the Studio maintained a decidedly educational atmosphere. The members were still searching for and developing their artistic talents. Furthermore, the studio members were involved in the great social works which occupied the hearts and minds of many Russians, taking time and energy away from their theatrical studies. Often, in the first years following the Revolution, the actors of the Second Studio performed for the workers in local factories. These were heady times for the young actors, as R. N. Molchanova relates:

> We played in cold, unheated facilities. The audience, sitting in their coats, in felt boots, most actively participated in the course of the performance, often loudly responding to one or another event. But this didn't bother us since we felt the enormous first-hand interest of the audience in all that was happening on the stage, we saw hundreds of warm, bright eyes, eager for knowledge, fixed on us (qtd. in Vinogradskaya 386).[4]

These early experiences served as excellent training for the young Studio members, offering them the opportunity to perform classic roles for enthusiastic audiences while strengthening their skills as performers. At the same time they were able to answer Lunacharsky's call for active participation in the education of the masses.

Along with plays and concerts, the Second Studio prepared several special programs centered around political themes for performance in factories and clubs. In the winter of 1918/19 the Studio presented fifteen regional concerts in conjunction with lectures by Moscow University professor P. N. Sakulin. For these performances the Studio prepared pieces by Gogol, Nekrasov, Koltsov, Nikitin, and Chekhov. Such performances were always well received by the workers for whom they were prepared.

As the Studio members gained experience in their first years, they began to look for plays to produce. They were primarily interested at this time in plays which, like *The Green Ring*, relied on atmosphere more than on any particularly innovative form. This preference was clearly demonstrated by two productions which followed *The Green Ring: Youth* (*Младость*) by L. Andreev in 1918 and *The Rose Pattern* (*Узор из роз*) by F. Sologub in 1920, both of which capitalized on the youthful energy of the Studio.

In the early years of the Revolution and Civil War, there were few inherently political plays available for production. Immediately following the revolution only a small number of writers, most notably the Futurists, wrote plays celebrating the event. This did not mean there was no demand for such plays. On the contrary, the years following the revolution saw a veritable theatrical epidemic as new amateur and professional companies sprang up everywhere. These companies "enthusiastically performed the classical plays as well as they could, but their productions were usually of a propagandist nature" (*Russian and Soviet Theater* 44).

The propagandist nature of the new theatres, however, had not yet reached the established companies which were still oriented toward a classical repertoire. The long established, traditional theatres resisted the move away from the theatrical forms which had been so successful before the revolution. In general they perceived their role in the new order as that of preservation for the purpose of introducing the proletariat to the "spiritual richness" which had not previously been available to either workers or peasants (*Russian and Soviet Theater* 46). In line with the desire to preserve what had been effective in the past while moving gently toward the future, the decision was made by the Second Studio to offer a new play by Leonid Andreev, *Youth*.

Andreev was not a newcomer to the Moscow Art Theatre. Early in the century he had written thirty plays in the Symbolist style and for a time was one of the most popular dramatists in Russia. At that time, Stanislavsky had been quite enthusiastic about the possibilities he saw in Symbolist drama and in 1907 the Moscow Art Theatre produced Andreev's *The Life of Man*. The production was most notable for its staging which featured black velvet draperies with outlines of doors and windows in white rope. Although the production was very popular, it did not remain long in the repertoire, due to Stanislavsky's belief that the play was too abstract to allow the actors to create living characters.

Andreev's play *Youth* had been offered to the Moscow Art Theatre in November, 1916, but it had not yet been produced. Andreev himself was quite eager for the production, and offered the piece to Nemirovich-Danchenko *gratis*. This play was a return to an earlier style of writing for the playwright. Before 1906, Andreev had been a realistic writer and it was in this vein that *Youth* was written. A story of young people coming of age, *Youth* revisited many of the themes found in *The Green Ring* such as the search for happiness and preparation for the future. It also offered characters similar to those with which the studio members had already known popular success. After its debut on December 13, 1918, *Youth* became a part of the Studio repertoire until 1925 and was considered to be one of its best pieces of work. It was not enough, however, to revive Andreev's flagging career as a playwright and his reputation declined.

The director's duties for *Youth* were assumed by N. N. Litovtseva and V. L. Mchedelov. They were assisted by Stanislavsky who, after attending a rehearsal of the second act, stepped in to reshape the performances. Stanislavsky felt the directors had relied on soft sentimentality when what was called for was a more vigorous portrayal of the youthful thirst for life (Vinogradskaya 386).

Stanislavsky's influence on the production was profound, even though he never attended a full rehearsal. For this play he worked with the principal actors at his home, helping them to find a sense of honesty and significance in support of the theme of the play as it coincided with the concerns of the studio: the problems of modern youth in a time of social upheaval. This was also the theme of Solugub's *The Rose Pattern*. Both of these plays are characteristic of the formative period of the Studio, what Stanislavsky referrred to as the "childhood" of the group, the four years from 1916–1920 (Ivanov 106).

During this early period in the life of the Studio the members were indoctrinated into both the ethics and aesthetics of the Art Theatre by their teachers. The Second Studio was a demanding school and the students were not coddled by their instructors. In her memoirs, Maria Knebel' recalls the rules of the Studio in the following way:

> It was left up to us to chart our own paths. In the Studio, there was a law the justice of which I understood much later: to teach is impossible, but to learn is possible. And another law: display initiative. No one can do anything for you unless you yourself put into the work the whole measure of your soul, talent, resourcefulness, unless you yourself look for scenes, prepare them,

show yourself etc. But if you will take the initiative and be persistent, then you will always receive the advice and help you need (144).[5]

In accordance with these policies, the teachers at the Second Studio assisted with scenes only after the initial work had been done by the students and then only if the scenes, as shown to the teachers, were well done and interesting. Only twice every season were these scenes shown to the teachers, and on these showings rested the fates of the young actors.

One of the most influential teachers for whom scenes were prepared was Elizaveta S. Telesheva who trained the Studio members in Stanislavsky's "system," with particular attention to work on the self. Knebel' describes Telesheva, for whom she had the greatest respect, in the following terms:

> A not particularly gifted actress, she was an exceptionally subtle and talented mentor of young actors. She was able to be an actor's genuine friend, perceptive, but not sensitive in a negative sense, attentive but not sentimental, able to see in the duckling the future swan and to help with its birth. Like no one else, she was able to help with the complex process of crystallization going on in the soul of the future actor, to imbue it with the highest ethical aesthetic standards. When the soul is athirst, that is when this imbuing is needed. She knew how to do this with great tact (145).[6]

Classes in other disciplines were offered to the students by a variety of teachers. Among them were classes in diction offered by N. A. Podgornii and E. F. Saricheva, dancing taught by A. M. Shalomitova, and rhythm as taught by Stanislavsky's brother, V. S. Alekseev. Voice class was offered by the director of the Moscow Art Theatre chorus, M. E. Piatnitskii and acrobatics, considered one of the most important disciplines of the theatre, was taught by V. A. Zhanto.

Knebel' also credits much of her training to Mchedelov, the founder of the Studio and the man she refers to as "the studio's soul" (145). It was with Mchedelov that the Studio members studied the art of improvisation, a crucial element in the preparation of the Studio's 1922 production of *The Story of Ivan the Fool and his Two Brothers (Сказка об Иване дураке и его двух братьях: Семене-воине и Тарасе-брюхане, и немой сестре Маланье, и о старом дьяволе и трех чертенятах).*[7]

Adapted from a story by Lev Tolstoy, the production of *Ivan the Fool* was a collaborative effort by all the greatest talents of the Moscow Art Theatre community. Among those who worked on the production were Evgenii Vakhtangov, Stanislavsky and Mikhail Chekhov, who also wrote the adaptation.

Ivan the Fool offered broad possibilities for the director's imagination both in staging and characterization and at one time or another all three, Vakhtangov, Stanislavsky and Chekhov, had a hand in its development. This fanciful tale of country folk and devils was a departure from the previous successes of the Second Studio. In contrast to the sentimental realism of *The Green Ring* and *Youth*, *Ivan the Fool* featured stylized characters, costumes and make-up. Unfortunately, this change was not well received by the audience, which had come to expect something quite different from the Second Studio. Ivanova characterizes this crucial moment in the Studio's life as follows:

> The period of work on the play took too long—directors changed, and therefore the performance, brilliantly realized in its separate parts had no unity of overall concept. Furthermore, over the four years of its life, the studio had already formed its audience, which wanted offerings along the lines of *The Green Ring* and *Youth*. The transition from the psychological intimate-chamber plays, to a show that made use of conventional, crude devices turned out to be unexpected and undesirable. Nevertheless it was *Ivan the Fool* that became the turning point in the transition of the studio from childhood to maturity. The chance, in the course of long, first-hand work to rub shoulders with such master directors as Vakhtangov and Stanislavsky, with such a teacher as M. A. Chekhov, [as well as] the search for the form of the performance, the stage presentation of the uninhibited folk imagination—all of this does not pass without leaving a trace and makes you grow up whether you want to or not (107).[8]

And with this growth came the inevitable dreams of independence among some members of the Studio. Conditions at the Moscow Art Theatre in 1922, however, did not permit a move away from the parent organization.

That year, 1922, was one of many changes in the Moscow theatrical scene. First, the tremendous success of Vakhtangov's *Princess Turandot* at the Third Studio of the Moscow Art Theatre, which had recently been assimilated into the Moscow Art Theatre community, caused a great sensation in theatrical circles with its blend of fantastic settings and truthful acting.[9] Further excitement was aroused at this time by the innovative work of Meyerhold and Tairov. In 1922 Meyerhold produced *The Magnificent Cuckhold* bringing to the stage for the first time his experiments in biomechanics and constructivism. At the same time Tairov's Kamerny Theatre began to find success with architectural settings for more classical pieces, placing traditional literature within a cubist-expressionist environment.

In the Autumn of the year, Stanislavsky took a large group from the Moscow Art Theatre community on a tour of Europe and America, leaving the Theatre and the Studios under the supervision of Nemirovich-Danchenko. As Ivanova notes, "Left on its own, the Second Studio was carried away by experiments and searches...." (107).[10] There occurred a period of reorganization within the Moscow Art Theatre community and the Studio was no longer under the close supervision of experienced veterans but was under the leadership of a group of five young members: Vershilov, Sudakov, Kaluzhskii, Batalov and Verbitskii.

What followed was what Stanislavsky would refer to, in 1924, as the Second Studio's "orgy of futurism" (Smeliansky 43). The Studio's 1923 productions of Schiller's *The Robbers (Die Raubers)* and Ostrovsky's *Storm (Гроза)* came to signify a move away from the traditions of the Moscow Art Theatre and towards the work of Meyerhold and Tairov.

Invested in the concepts for these productions were the Studio members' own desires for artistic and social liberation. The young artists saw in these plays an inherent human desire for freedom from the demands of both nature and society which echoed their own desires for freedom from the traditions of the Moscow Art Theatre.

For their audience, however, the artists' visions were far from realized. The production values of *The Robbers* were eclectic and confusing to the spectators, who were presented with a strange mix of the real and the fantastic. The cubist-constructivist set was combined with realistic costumes. The make-up for the production was basically realistic, but applied in such a way as to make the actors' faces appear deformed. The play itself was adapted by P. Antokolskii who transformed Schiller's prose into verse and added an epilogue.

Knebel' makes the assertion that perhaps the primary difficulty with the production of *The Robbers* was rooted in the Studio's training. She believes that the Studio members had studied the lessons of Stanislavsky, Luzhskii and Mchedelov too well to ignore their foundation in realism and as a result their attempt to place contemporary leftist sensibilities on the stage could only fail. These attributes of the production simply were not aesthetically appropriate as performed by the Studio members and should not have been incorporated into the production (163).

The Studio's interpretation of Ostrovsky's classic play was similarly received by its audiences, which had difficulty understanding what the young artists were trying to accomplish. *The Robbers* and *Storm* were not total failures, however, since they brought to the attention of the critics the talents of four actors who would become very important to the second generation of the Moscow Art Theatre: Batalov, Khmelyov, Azarine and Prudkin.

Among these young actors, Nikolai Khmelyov was particularly noteworthy. Knebel' writes of him very favorably, praising even his earliest work. Khmelyov's acting talent came to the fore in his portrayal of Spiegelberg in *The Robbers*. His embodiment of the character was so complete that, when referring to the stylized make-up used in the production, Knebel' asserts that "It seemed that together with his face, Khmelyov made for himself a new soul, a new way of thinking" (165).[11]

This mastery of the actor's art was surprising to many of the more seasoned performers in the Moscow Art Theatre community. Knebel' expresses their feelings in the following way:

> It was incomprehensible how this barely full grown young actor, almost a boy, who had grown up in a workers' suburb, shy and unsociable, made the extremely complicated inner world of Spiegelberg absolutely his own as if he had experienced it in its most insignificant details. How did he achieve such all encompassing belief in his own chosenness, in his uniqueness, in the fact that he and no other was foreordained by a higher power to lead the crowd behind him into an unknown kingdom(165).[12]

This exceptional talent for characterization was the hallmark of Khmelyov's brilliant career. He later became a member of the governing board of the Second Studio and served as the artistic director of the Moscow Art Theatre from 1943–1945. Sadly, his career was cut short when he died on the stage of the Moscow Art in 1945 at the age of forty-four.

The talent of the young actors could not, however, bring success to *The Robbers*. It was especially unpopular with Nemirovich-Danchenko, who wrote to Stanislavsky in March of 1923:

> The Second Studio has produced *The Robbers*. Independently....I did not hide that the play was decidedly not to my taste....Something about the production is unpleasant. Deliberate leftism, superficial, nonsensical, cheap, that is, constructivism, monsters instead of people etc....The actors as actors are not bad...but the external form [of the production] is unpleasant (qtd. in Knebel' 167).[13]

Clearly, the production failed to find favor with the administration of the Moscow Art Theatre.

Nemirovich-Danchenko was less negative, however, about the Studio's production of *Storm*. Even though the style of *Storm* was very similar to that of *The Robbers*, Nemirovich-Danchenko believed in the production, perhaps because it promised to find its ground somewhere closer to the middle than did *The Robbers*. The work did not, however, go smoothly. Nemirovich-Danchenko and Sudakov, who directed the piece, believed that the classic could be staged in such a way that it could overcome the specificity of time and place inherent in the text and speak to the new Russian audience.

The concept for the production was Sudakov's. He wanted to remove the piece from any specific time or place and emphasize the eternal and universal aspects of the characters. The play was performed before an abstract background and enhanced with music in the hopes that the poetic aspects of the production would shine through. Unfortunately for the participants, these hopes were not realized and the production was given only 45 performances before being removed from the repertoire in 1924.

The last independent project of the Second Studio was begun in the summer of 1924. It was a production of *Elizabeth Petrovna* (*Елизавета Петровна*) by D. P. Smolina, under the direction of Mchedelov and L. V. Baratov. This project was never completed, due to the untimely death of Mchedelov. With the death of its founder and principal leader, the Second Studio began to lose its direction and entered a period of transition. At this time it was decided that the Second Studio would be assimilated into the Moscow Art Theatre proper.

The entire Moscow Art Theatre community was in a state of upheaval coinciding with the return of the touring company from the United States. This touring company included a large number of the performers who had served for many years as the core of talent for the Moscow Art Theatre. Also included in this group were a few of the younger members who had come out of the studios. During the two years that these performers and Stanislavsky were on tour, Nemirovich-Danchenko had continued to operate the Moscow Art Theatre with those who had remained behind, relying heavily on the studios and their members to perform in the places of those who were absent. During these years, Nemirovich-Danchenko also came to believe that the time was right for the Moscow Art Theatre to undergo a major reorganization.

In the spring of 1924, Nemirovich-Danchenko was searching for the correct path down which to lead the Moscow Art Theatre. He was trying to see ahead in order to anticipate the future and the Art Theatre's place in it. He was closely watching Meyerhold on one end of the spectrum and the conservative Maly Theatre on the other, hoping to find some answers to his questions, many of which concerned repertoire.

As a successful playwright himself, Nemirovich-Danchenko knew that a new age such as the one Moscow was experiencing demanded a new literature. He understood that the repertoire which had served the Moscow Art Theatre well in the past was inappropriate for, if not incomprehensible to, the new Russian audience. Smeliansky quotes a letter Nemirovich-Danchenko wrote at this time expressing his concern.

It's no good even thinking about *Uncle Vanya*. *Three Sisters* would be a joke both in terms of the content and of the *age* of the actors and actresses. *The Cherry Orchard* would be banned, or rather they would ban the lamenting of the estates of the gentry, and the play can't be staged from a different "Hello, new life!" angle. *Ivanov* is so out of sympathy with an optimistic age as to be incomprehensible (42).

Nemirovich-Danchenko also knew that decisive action was needed in order to save the life of the Moscow Art Theatre and prevent it from following the deadening path of the conservative Maly Theatre.

Such a decisive action was taken in the spring and summer of 1924, just before the return of Stanislavsky and the touring company. Smeliansky characterizes Nemirovich-Danchenko's actions as: "Vested with dictatorial powers, he tackled head-on what had been one of the Theatre's main ongoing problems since the revolution: what to do about the Studios. In the process he decided the future direction of the Art Theatre itself" (42). What followed was the complete re-organization of the Moscow Art Theatre and its studios.

Nemirovich-Danchenko negotiated the re-organization with Anatoly V. Lunacharsky, who was the People's Commissar for Education, along with Olga Malinovskaya, who had charge of what were then called the Academic theatres which included the newly re-named Moscow Art Academic Theatre. Officials of Narkompros, the People's Commissariat for Education, were also involved in the negotiations. All of those concerned felt that the relationship of the Moscow Art Theatre to the various studios was a major consideration in the proposed changes.

Nemirovich-Danchenko's secretary, Olga Bokshanskaya, was travelling with Stanislavsky and the touring company and kept Nemirovich apprised of events occurring overseas. In a letter to Bokshanskaya dated February 10–15, 1924, Nemirovich-Danchenko presented the newly negotiated plan as follows:

I need the *unconditional* agreement of K. S. and the shareholders to my plan (that is the one I have worked out).

Or everything will be left to chance: to a decision by Narkompros or the authorities, or, if nobody pushes us, we will decide the future in September (!!!) or I will decide here by myself...

Should the 1st Studio take the New Theatre...it will be more inclined to be completely independent (2nd Art Theatre?). Especially [Michael] Chekhov. He has his own artistic-ethical line and is afraid of being swamped by other elements. But Chekhov doesn't meet with total sympathy. As he says, one third of the studio treats him "rather negatively." And if the 2nd group (the veterans) suddenly start to come together with the former theatre, well then splits might start to appear in the 1st Studio and one or two might be drawn towards us.

The 2nd Studio is in such a state that the authorities are amazed I should defend it. I think I can reform it and retain the core.

The 3rd Studio, although it came a cropper with "Marriage," still holds together *as a studio*.

The 4th will be left to survive as it wishes. It attracts sympathy...

At all events I would add that by "unconditional" I mean that not all those who are currently in America may prove to be essential to us in Moscow. I would put it like this, that in the New Art Theatre we have *absolutely no need* of artists (*or staff*) who have proved themselves to be undisciplined, unethical and completely badly behaved (*Moscow Art Theatre Letters* 324).

The tone of Nemirovich-Danchenko's correspondence during the American tour, such as in the above letter, clearly shows that the stress exerted by social, political and financial pressures was taking a toll.

Nemirovich was not alone in his frustrations during this time of change and uncertainty. Almost since the first days of the Civil War, Stanislavsky had begun to feel at odds with his students and colleagues. He felt beseiged by the new trends in theatricalized theatre as practiced by Meyerhold and Tairov. Meyerhold, who had been a close associate of Stanislavsky at the turn of the century, wanted now to close the Moscow Art Theatre (*Moscow Art Theatre Letters* 315). For several years before his death in 1922, Vakhtangov, who also favored more stylized productions, had urged Stanislavsky to leave the Moscow Art Theatre and its traditions for the sake of his artistic soul. By 1923 each of the studios had experimented with new forms and had moved away from the traditions of the Moscow Art Theatre. Stanislavsky perceived these experiments as a personal affront and felt that his students had betrayed him and his teaching.

Stanislavsky's reaction to Nemirovich-Danchenko's plan is contained in a letter from Konstantin Sergeevich to Nemirovich, dated June 10, 1924. In it he compares himself to King Lear making the studios his faithless daughters, a correlation he would make on more than one occasion. In his letter he states:

I accept and approve the measures you have taken. The 1st Studio—to be independent. This long-standing sickness of my soul requires a definite operation. (A pity that it will be called the 2nd MXT. It has betrayed it in every respect). Privately I call the studio Goneril's Studio.

The 3rd Studio also to separate—I approve. That is Regan's Studio. The Second Studio can be likened to Cordelia. They are nice and there is something better in them but, but...you know them better at the moment, I, at a distance, cannot conceive what they will make of themselves after their Futuristic spree...

If it is still possible to save the Art Theatre then only one man can do it, you. I am powerless. My edge has gone completely. For two years I've had to shout and swear so much that now I have no authority of any kind while you, on the other hand, have acquired more... [...]

Be the leading personality in the Studio? Fine. I agree and will try to do what I can. But this time you sustain a belief or even some sort of ray of hope in me for the Studio. They have disappointed me so much that I have no more belief in them or good feelings towards them. All the people in the studios are petit bourgeois with tiny, practical, utilitarian spiritual needs. There is a touch of art here and there and a lot of compromises...

I am almost incapable of reaching compromises and when I do they credit them to my account, exploit my weakness and abuse it. And when I stand firm they say I am intolerable and run away. Nobody needs what I have to give... (*Moscow Art Theatre Letters* 324–325).

Stanislavsky was understandably exhausted and disillusioned when he returned from America, as this letter shows. The tour had initially been undertaken in the hopes of raising some capital in foreign currency. While the first half of the tour had been a success with sell-out crowds, the decision to remain abroad for a second year had been a grave mistake. The novelty of the Moscow Art Theatre in America had faded and by the time the troupe returned to Moscow it was $25,000.00 in debt. The stresses of touring, furthermore, had caused relationships within the ensemble to weaken as money became tight and tempers flared. When word reached Stanislavsky that reports had appeared in the Russian press accusing the company of "having sold out on the Revolution, of living a high life while fellow countrymen starved" he was appalled. The final blow came when he realized that "even Nemirovich fell prey to these suspicions" (*Moscow Art Theatre Letters* 316).

Two years later, in 1926, Stanislavsky expressed in *My Life in Art* what seems to be the fundamental frustration he was feeling during this transition period. He felt that the new generation of theatre artists were trying to circumvent the natural evolution of their art, pushing too quickly what should be allowed to move slowly. He accused the new generation of impatience which "violates art, stuffing it with sharpness of form and content." He denied the constructivists' concept of simplicity, declaring that the platforms and machines on which they performed disturbed the eye "even more than the colorful luxury and richness of production." He staunchly believed that "a time will come when the evolution of art shall have completed its predestined circle and nature itself will teach us methods and technique for the interpretation of the sharpness of the new life" (566–567). In August, 1924, Konstantin Sergeevich was too tired to fight with the new generation any longer and so the relationship of the Moscow Art Theatre to its studios changed.

When all negotiations were concluded and the re-organization actually occurred, there were some members of the Third Studio who joined with the Second Studio, his "Cordelia," to become the Dramatic Studio and School, with Stanislavsky in charge. These students were now to be involved solely in main-house productions, performing small parts and walk-ons. It was some time before this second generation would in reality be fully encompassed by the Moscow Art Theatre.

As time passed, Stanislavsky's publicly expressed sentiments were more positive about the new arrangements than were those expressed in his private correspondence. On December 27, 1926, more than two years after the re-organization, Konstantin Sergeevich returned to the image of Lear in a speech marking the tenth anniversary of the founding of the Second Studio. In that speech he said:

> Today I feel like King Lear, who lost all of his daughters and, finally, in his old age is reunited with his favorite Cordelia.
>
> Indeed, today we celebrate three great joys. First, the joining of the Second studio. Second, returning to the womb, not to say the bastard son, but the prodigal through all the ins and outs and trends of our complicated, entangled and changeable art. And the third joy, that today accomplishes the merger of the youths with the oldsters. This—a great pleasure, a great holiday for all of us, "oldsters", and, specifically, for me, who has long worked on the creation of this studio.
>
> The idea is simple. To allow the old wisdom to direct the young courage and strength, to allow the young courage and strength to support the old wisdom. Only under such aesthetic conditions can our work flourish and own the future...
>
> Therefore the Second studio, which successively appears to follow these traditions of theatre, must return to this important mission not only for our theater, but for Russian art (*Papers, Speeches, Interviews and Letters* 271).

With these stirring words of support, both the members of the Second Studio and the Moscow Art Theatre could feel vindicated in their acceptance of their new relationship.

The first decisive step towards assimilation into the parent organization had come with the production of *The Days of the Turbins* by Mikhail Bulgakov. Adapted from Bulgakov's novel *The White Guard*, *The Days of the Turbins* was the first real success of the new generation following its acceptance into the main house of the Moscow Art. It also marked the beginning of a long and difficult association between the Theatre and the writer.

In January of 1925, Bulgakov, of his own volition, began an adaptation for the stage of his partially published novel. Then in April of 1925 he was invited to meet with Boris Vershilov to discuss the possibility of a production by the rejuvenated Moscow Art Theatre.

The Moscow Art Theatre's new literary director, Pavel Markov, was searching for ways to revive the Art Theatre repertoire with new plays by new playwrights. He decided to support a production of *The White Guard*. This decision coincided with yet another revamping of the Art Theatre, this time of its internal administrative structure.

In September of 1925 the administrative side of the Moscow Art Theatre was organized into a parliamentary type structure consisting of two chambers. The upper chamber included Stanislavsky, Leonidov, Kachalov, Moskvin and Luzhskii. The lower chamber contained primarily young people under the chairmanship of Markov. Initially the members of the lower chamber were Ilya Sudakov, Boris Vershilov, Nikolai Gorchakov, Iuri Zavadskii, Evgenii Kaluzhskii, Mark Prudkin and Nikolai Batalov. This group, which had considerable powers in matters of repertoire, announced its decision to produce *The White Guard* in October, 1925 (Smeliansky 49).

Unfortunately, the enthusiasm of the young people was not sufficient to overcome objections to the play expressed by, among others, Stanislavsky and Lunacharsky. In a letter to Luzhskii dated October 12, 1925, Lunacharsky wrote:

> I have read the play "The White Guard" attentively. I find nothing inadmissable in it from the political point of view but I cannot conceal my own personal opinion. I consider Bulgakov to be a very talented man but this play of his is exceptionally undistinguished except for the one or two lively scenes of the Hetman's departure. All the rest is either the turmoil of war or unusually commonplace, rather stupidly dull scenes of middle-class philistinism of no interest to anyone. There is not one single character, not one engaging situation and the end simply makes one angry with its vagueness and total lack of effect (*Moscow Art Theatre Letters* 327).

These were discouraging words for the young actors who believed that in Bulgakov they had found a new Chekhov.

What followed were many revisions and compromises, something the members of the second generation would soon learn was inevitable in the Russia of that day. Smeliansky describes Bulgakov's efforts to make his play acceptable to those in control of the project, both internal and external to the theatre itself.

> He threw his prose into the crucible of the theatre and brought the Art
> Theatre not a play but molten lava which it still remained to pour into some
> kind of mould. The junior members of the Art Theatre had no specifically
> Bulgakovian mould at their disposal. The model Sudakov knew was the tried
> and trusted form of classical Chekhovian drama, and into this mould the
> Theatre and its playwright duly poured *The White Guard*. Much would not fit
> and had to be abandoned. Inevitably there was a price to pay…The play was
> a staggering success, but its author went unmentioned in accounts of that
> success for several decades (65).

The price of compromise was paid not only by Bulgakov, but by the
young actors as well. They began the project believing that their cooperation with government officials would lead those officials to make
some concessions in the future. This expectation, as they soon learned,
was not to be fulfilled. *The Days of the Turbins* was a popular success
but it did not win greater autonomy for the company which continued to
suffer under close government scrutiny. The true cost of their
compromises became even clearer in the next production of the second
generation, *Armoured Train 14–69*.

The Moscow Art Theatre proposed a production of *Armoured Train
14–69* as part of the celebrations surrounding the tenth anniversary of
the October Revolution. The play, based on a novella by Vsevelod
Ivanov, was meant to be a celebration of the power of the people. For
this reason Stanislavsky undertook to adapt the novella during the
rehearsal process, envisioning the piece as "not so much *for* the Theatre
as *in and by* the Theatre" (Polyakova 316). This production was
particularly important in terms of the assimilation of the Second Studio
into the body of the Moscow Art Theatre. *Armoured Train 14–69*
marked the first time both generations worked together to develop a
piece and, in the course of rehearsals, Stanislavsky had an opportunity to
work with the veterans using the methods with which the Studio
members were already familiar.

The story of the play is one of revolution and counter-revolution,
peasants, gentry and the White Army, and centers around the capture of
an armoured train by partisans. What was meant as a glorious tribute to
the spirit of the October Revolution soon became yet another point of
conflict, this time not only between the Moscow Art Theatre and the
Soviet government, but between Stanislavsky and his actors of both
generations.

Originally, supervision of the adaptation was assigned to Markov
and Sudakov. Rehearsals of crowd scenes were held by Sudakov and
everything else was rehearsed by Litovtseva. With these arrangements in
place, Stanislavsky left on a tour to Leningrad where he was introduced
to the painter Chupiatov who had done some designs for the ballet.

Konstantin Sergeevich admired the artist's work and engaged him to design *Armoured Train*. Unfortunately, when the preliminary sketches arrived in Moscow in August, Stanislavsky was dissatisfied. It was necessary to begin again, although time was running perilously short. Chupiatov was replaced by Viktor Simov.

At the same time, the Glavrepertkom or Central Repertory Committee began causing difficulties, demanding a large number of changes, including a complete reworking of the final act. This situation was complicated by the fact that Ivanov was abroad and unavailable to address the problem areas. Work continued, nevertheless, and Stanislavsky saw a run-through of several scenes on October 3. The first complete run-through, which was staged for the benefit of the Repertkom, was held on October 31 in the foyer of the theatre, without costumes or make-up. By this time Stanislavsky had become quite dissatisfied with the production and stepped in to fix what he could.

His first concern was that Litovtseva had taken too soft a tone for the play, especially the opening scene. Senior members of the company such as Vishnievski and Olga Knipper reverted to past experience, producing a "Chekhovian softness" similar to that which Stanislavsky had fought against in *The Days of the Turbins*. He was looking for murderous hate from actors who were unwilling to appear unsympathetic in their roles as White refugees. They were toning down the characters and failing to provide strong positive actions. Benedetti points to the political aspect of this difficulty. "At the root of the problem lay a degree of political anxiety. They did not, as artists, wish to be identified with the characters they were playing, something which is not unknown. Stanislavski (*sic*) understood but would have none of it" (281).

In the end, Stanislavsky, using a favorite strategy, created a physical problem for the actors. He made them fight the furniture. Polyakova relates the event in the following manner, quoting Gorchakov's rehearsal notes:

> ...Stanislavsky began: "Now let's correct the physical self-awareness of the actors in this episode. Move in the greenhouse walls; push all the objects on top of each other—the furniture, the crates, the bundles. I'll ask you all to clamber onto anything you like: the back of chairs, what was once a piano crate, a pile of books, tumbled about or trussed up. Help Olga Leonardovna climb onto the back of some sturdy armchair..."
>
> The cosy greenhouse began to look like a cluttered hen-coop and the "last remnants of the Russian intelligentsia" like bedraggled chickens.
>
> Olga Leonardovna, perched on the back of a large sofa, was valiant enough to protest: "Look here, this is really uncomfortable."
>
> "That is exactly how it should feel," K.S. replied promptly. "They're all very uncomfortable too."

"But, honestly, one feels such an ass!" Olga Leonardovna persisted.

"Splendid!" K.S. egged her on. "They all feel completely absurd. Only you hide from everyone that you feel like an ass and that's why you have to talk about planning to line the greenhouse with silk..." (318).

This rehearsal was successful in that it made the actors feel "as they should, in moving them away from the 'naturalness' that they easily—too easily, in Stanislavsky's opinion—fell into" (Polyakova 318).

The success of Stanislavsky's technique was only temporary, however, since the actors soon became accustomed to their shaky perches and fell back into their earlier performances, despite Konstantin Sergeevich's suggestions that they constantly change the way the furniture was stacked in order to maintain the feeling of unpredictability in their surroundings. Stanislavsky found similar difficulties in the crowd scenes as rehearsed by Sudakov.

During his reworking of the crowd scenes, Konstantin Sergeevich used a technique which came to be known as "Here, Today, Now" in which he asked the actors questions about what they would do under the given circumstances. In the case of *Armoured Train*, he removed a serious block when he imitated Lunacharsky in the following exercise:

Comrade actors of the Art Theatre, in order to defend the Soviet state against the most recent attacks by our capitalist enemies, you must go with me immediately to the broadcasting station and tell the whole world that the rumour in the bourgeois press that the Art Theatre has refused to play *The Armoured Train* is a base, common lie. Who's coming with me? (qtd. in Benedetti 282).

The actors responded and rehearsals continued with renewed vigor.

Armoured Train 14–69 opened on November 8, 1927, in a gala performance. There was no doubt as to who was truly responsible for the final outcome of the production, even though, of 76 rehearsals, Stanislavsky had taken only eleven, four of which were run-throughs and seven which were of individual scenes. The play was enthusiastically received by both the public and the authorities. Lunacharsky saw the production as proof that the Art Theatre had finally moved into the new era, using high art to illuminate the revolution.

For the actors, the impact of *Armoured Train* was less positive. What was a triumph for Soviet literature, Soviet theatre and socialist realism forced the actors to "betray themselves as artists but not as revolutionaries," which was especially harmful for the older generation and set the stage for a life of disillusionment for the second generation which would continue to work under heavy government control (Smeliansky personal interview).

Perhaps most importantly, *Armoured Train 14–69* marks the moment when the Second Studio became truly assimilated by the Moscow Art Theatre. This production employed the talents of both generations working together, and from that time on it became increasingly difficult to distinguish the two as separate entities. What had begun as a group of enthusiastic young people, eager to perfect their craft under the leadership of the master, had become a cadre of disillusioned and disappointed political tools who would be known for their role in the "sovietization" of the Moscow Art Theatre rather than for their accomplishments as artists.

Stanislavsky with the cast of *The Green Ring*, 1916

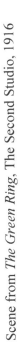

Scene from *The Green Ring*, The Second Studio, 1916

A. K. Tarasova as Finochka in *The Green Ring*

N. P Batalov and V. E. Sokolova in *Youth*, 1918

V. Ia. Stanitsin in make-up for *The Robbers*, 1923

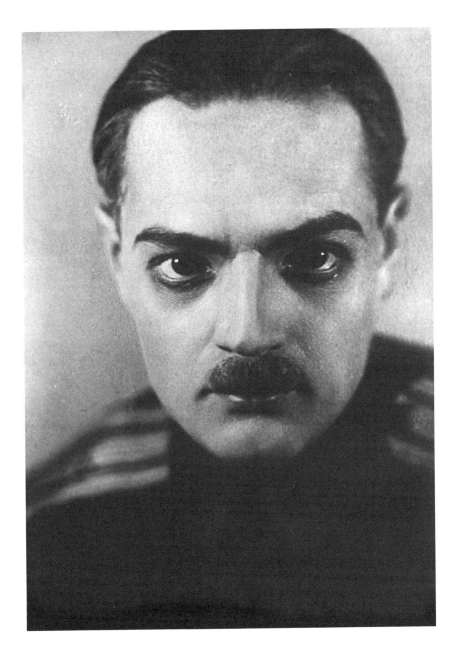

N. P. Khmelyov as Aleksei Turbin in *The Days of the Turbins*

Act III, Scene I, *The Days of the Turbins*

CHAPTER FOUR

The Third Studio:
The Rebellion of Vakhtangov

The Third Studio of the Moscow Art Theatre was almost entirely the creation of one man: Evgenii Bogrationovich Vakhtangov. Any attempt to understand this studio both as a part of the Moscow Art Theatre tradition and as a force in Soviet and World theatre must center on a study of the man himself. Vakhtangov was born on February 1, 1883, and died on May 29, 1922. "Between these two dates lies a brilliant, talented life, full of creative fire and genuine inspiration" (Kuza 5).[1]

Vakhtangov was born in Vladikavkaz into the wealthy family of a tobacco merchant.[2] He spent his childhood surrounded by family arguments and adults who, he believed, did not understand him in the least. He was very unhappy living with his cold and often angry father. Evgenii Bogrationovich was the eldest of four children and as such often bore the brunt of his father's rages. At the age of ten Vakhtangov entered the gymnasium, where he found refuge in the noisy life of other young people (Khersonsky 10–20). While still in school, Vakhtangov began to express his love for the theatre, participating in both private and public amateur performances.

In 1903, upon completion of his studies at the gymnasium, Vakhtangov entered Moscow University in the Natural Science department. A year later he transferred to the Law division, but the young man soon lost interest in this course of study. In the short time he had been in Moscow, Vakhtangov had found his true university in the Moscow Art Theatre.

During the 1903–1904 season of the Moscow Art Theatre, Vakhtangov became enthralled with the productions he attended, including Chekhov's *The Cherry Orchard (Вишневый сад)* and Gorky's *The Lower Depths (На дне.)* He also saw Gorky's *Small People (Мещане)*, *The Power of Darkness (Власть тьмы)* by Lev Tolstoy, *Pillars of Society* by Ibsen and Shakespeare's *Julius Caesar*. The young Vakhtangov was so inspired by these performances that he felt he must, for the sake of his soul, join this "brightly illuminated world, where life and fantasy are united and where the performer is merged in the creative impulse with the entire collective on the stage and with the audience in the hall" (Khersonsky 35).[3] The eager and inspired young artist saw in the famous theatre the emotional home for which he had long been searching.

Several years passed, however, before Vakhtangov occupied his artistic home. Before he could join the illustrious community at the Moscow Art Theatre he needed to study his craft—a learning process which began for Vakhtangov, as it has for many great theatre artists, in the realm of the amateur theatre. In the summer of 1904 he made his first foray into the world of the director, serving in that capacity for the Vladikavkaz Students' Workshop in Grozny. His directorial debut was a production of *Festival of Peace* (*Das Friedensfest*) by Hauptmann, a play he would direct again in the First Studio. In January, 1905, he directed *Pedagogics* by O. Erista for the Smolensko-Vyazemskoe Association of Countrymen at Moscow University. In both of these productions he did double duty, working both as an actor and as the director. In the Hauptmann piece he played Wilhelm and in *Pedagogics* he took the role of the pedagogue Flashman.

1905 was an important year for Vakhtangov, not only as an artist but also as a man, for on October 9 of that year he married Nadezhda Mikhailovna Baitzurova. This appears to have been a stroke of good fortune for Vakhtangov, because for the rest of his life his wife quietly supported him in his almost obsessive search for a rejuvenated theatre. She also provided him with a much beloved son, Sergei, born on January 1, 1907.

In June, 1906, Vakhtangov organized the Vladikavkaz Students' Association. For this group he again served as director/actor, creating a production of *The Strong and The Weak* (*Сильные и Слабые*) by N. Timkovskii in which he played the role of Georgii Preturov.[4] In October of the same year he organized yet another theatrical group, the Drama Circle, composed of students from Moscow University. With this group he directed a production of *Summerfolk* (*Дачники*) by Maxim Gorky, in which he also played the role of Vlas. The role of Suslov was played by Boris Sushkevich, who would later join the Moscow Art Theatre and the First Studio.

Two years later, in 1908, Vakhtangov directed Gorky's *The Lower Depths* (*На Дне*) for the Vladikavkaz group, playing the role of the Baron. Then, in June 1909, he directed the play *Zinochka* by Sergei Nedolin at the Vladikavkaz Art-Drama Circle and again served also as an actor, playing the role of Magnitskii. Not only did he direct *Zinochka* in the summer of 1909, he also directed and performed in Hamsun's play *At the Gate of the Kingdom* (*У Врат Царства*) in which he played the role of Ivar Kareno, and directed a production of Chekhov's *Uncle Vanya* (*Дядя Ваня*) in which he played the role of Dr. Astrov.

Then, in August of that year, Vakhtangov took what would prove to be a defining step forward on his life's path. Against the wishes of his father, he left law school and entered Adashev's Drama School. Here he studied under Luzhskii, Leonidov, Kachalov, Glagol and other actors of the Moscow Art Theatre and gained the attention of one teacher in particular: Leopold Sulerzhitskii.

One characteristic of Vakhtangov's approach to theatre which impressed first Suler and then Nemirovich and Stanislavsky was his habit of keeping complete and accurate notes during rehearsals. This was an outgrowth of his years of work in the amateur theatre. As a director, Vakhtangov had always conducted extensive research for every production. He carefully developed each detail and did not limit himself to any single area of theatre craft, but became actively involved in every aspect of a production. He gave equal attention to script and character analyses, set design and construction, make-up, costumes and lighting. All creative elements were coordinated in order to support and reveal the underlying conceptual basis of the production and every aspect was carefully and thoroughly recorded in a meticulously written *regiebuch*. His 1909 production of *Zinochka*, for example, produced more than forty pages of preparatory work and directorial instruction. This thorough preparation led to polished productions which gained the enthusiastic support of critics and the admiration of his fellow students and teachers.

Vakhtangov made quick progress in his studies at the Adashev school. He was promoted to the second course in the winter of 1909–10. Then, in the summer of 1910, while working in Vladikavkaz, Vakhtangov received a telegram from his colleague L. I. Deikun who was preparing an audition for the Moscow Art Theatre and had lost her partner to illness. Vakhtangov answered her plea for help and returned to Moscow, where he quickly learned the role and substituted for the indisposed partner. His performance in this audition made such an impression that Nemirovich-Danchenko invited him to join the Moscow Art Theatre. Vakhtangov, however, wanted to finish his work at the school first and so declined the invitation, a decision supported by his teacher, Sulerzhitskii (Khersonsky 60–61).

As the end of 1910 approached, Suler was invited to direct a production of Maeterlinck's *The Blue Bird* at the Réjane theatre in Paris and he invited Vakhtangov to join him as his assistant. The trip to Paris opened Vakhtangov's eyes to many things. The vitality of the city, especially its night-life, excited him; but the French actors with whom he worked and the performances he attended left him quite disillusioned about the state of the theatre in Paris. He felt the actors were unprepared and unable to act, resorting to "disgusting and coarse declamation" (Vakhtangov qtd. in Khersonsky 72). In mid-February Vakhtangov returned to Moscow and on March 4 he joined the Moscow Art Theatre.

As a new member of the Moscow Art Theatre, Vakhtangov performed small roles in plays from the repertoire. He played the Gypsy in Tolstoy's *The Living Corpse (Живой труп,)* the Player-Queen in *Hamlet*, directed by Gordon Craig, and other minor roles. More importantly, Vakhtangov was groomed by Suler and Stanislavsky to become a teacher and when the First Studio was founded in October of 1912, Vakhtangov was given a great deal of responsibility for teaching his colleagues the use of Stanislavsky's "system." Stanislavsky had complete confidence in Vakhtangov, often stating that his student "knows how to teach my system better than I do" (Gorchakov qtd. in Orani 464). In the course of his teaching, however, Vakhtangov did not simply pass on the ideas of the master, but questioned everything, searching for ways to refine and perfect the "system."

Vakhtangov's sense of mission was very clear. Khersonsky quotes his diary for April 12, 1912:

> I want to form a studio, where we would be pupils. The principle [behind it]—is to try and achieve everything ourselves. The director is everyone. [I want] to test the system of K. S. on ourselves. [I want] to accept or reject it. [I want] to correct [it], to complete [it] or clear away the falsehood [from it]. Everyone who has entered the studio must love art in general and the stage in particular. [I want] to seek joy in creativity. [I want] to forget the public. To create for oneself. [I want us] to enjoy [art] for ourselves. [I want us] to be ourselves judges for ourselves (77).[5]

It was with these lofty goals in mind that Vakhtangov began his work which would, over the years, lead to a fuller understanding of Stanislavsky's theories as well as the emergence of Vakhtangov's own unique style.

As discussed in Chapter 2, *Holiday of Peace (Das Friedensfest)*, Vakhtangov's first directing project for the First Studio, was not met with unanimous approval. Following the controversy over this production Evgenii Bogrationovich decided to branch out on his own, establishing a new studio for amateur actors known as the Drama Studio.

This was the first of several independent groups with which he would work as founder, director or both up until the time of his death. And while Vakhtangov did not at this time end his relationship with the First Studio or the Moscow Art Theatre organization, the founding of the Drama Studio did, nevertheless, give him a measure of independence from his teachers and a greater opportunity to experiment with his own ideas, all of which eventually found their way back to his original artistic home.

Vakhtangov's unique relationship with the Moscow Art Theatre and its founders is characterized by Kuza in the following way. "Vakhtangov was a genuine son of the Art theatre, but a rebellious son. A spirit of epigonism,[6] a spirit of mindless and mechanical copying of the great masters was alien to Vakhtangov" (6).[7] His desire to fully understand, test and refine the "system" was what motivated Vakhtangov in his many experiments at the different studios. His independent work came full circle when, in 1920, the Drama Studio, also known as the Mansurovsky Studio after the name of the street where it was located, became the Third Studio of the Moscow Art Theatre.

As Vakhtangov continued to work at the several studios, teaching the "system" and directing productions, he came to feel that the primary shortcoming of the "system" and Stanislavsky's work was the loss of the theatrical. He believed that the theatre of Stanislavsky had, by striving for a photographic reflection of reality, ceased to exist as an art form. In a diary entry written at the All Saints Sanitorium on March 26, 1921, Vakhtangov describes what he sees as Stanislavsky's chief failing as an artist.

> Stanislavsky absolutely has not mastered theatrical form in the noblest meaning of the word. He is a master of images and unexpected devices of the living face. But absolutely not a master of form in theatrical presentation. Therefore, he killed theatre, took away flashy curtains, took away actors' entrances, took away the orchestra, took away all theatricality (qtd. in Rudnitsky "All Saints Notes" 150).[8]

Particularly in the era immediately following the 1917 Revolution, Vakhtangov felt the theatre needed "large, clear, graphic, but above all, theatrical motion" in response to the monumental nature of the times (Orani 469). His work moved steadily toward the grotesque and theatrical, as can be seen in his last and most noteworthy productions: Strindberg's *Erik XIV* at the First Studio, Ansky's *Dybbuk* at the Habima Theatre, and Maeterlinck's *Miracle of St. Anthony* and Gozzi's *Princess Turandot* at the Third Studio of the Moscow Art Theatre.

Chronologically, the first of these final productions was Maeterlinck's *Miracle of St. Anthony*. This production, which premiered on January 29, 1921, was the second time Vakhtangov directed the piece at his studio and according to Khersonsky, this second version was much better than the one staged in 1918 (224).[9] In the intervening years between the productions, Vakhtangov's personal outlook, always tending toward the critical, had become even more barbed. The original production showed a more gentle, forgiving interpretation of the bourgeois characters but the play received a very different, sharply satirical treatment in the second production. Vakhtangov's long-standing antipathy for the bourgeoisie strengthened during the years of the Revolution and Civil War and found an outlet for expression in this dark play by Maeterlinck. Simonov quotes Vakhtangov's expression of his post-revolution attitude as, "Now the theatrical means we use in *Miracle*—branding the bourgeoisie—concur with the demands of life in our time" (130).

The *Miracle of St. Anthony* is a study in contrasts and as such appealed greatly to Vakhtangov. The action of the play is a simple story which takes on a deeper meaning when viewed with Vakhtangov's eye for the grotesque. When the play opens, a simple, elderly housemaid is scrubbing the floor in a home where the wealthy mistress has recently died. The heirs are dining in the next room when, out of the pouring rain, a poor beggar arrives who reveals himself to be St. Anthony of Padua. He has been sent to bring the dead woman back to life, but conflict ensues when the heirs to the dead woman's fortune protest against her proposed resurrection. The stark contrast between the good-hearted maid, the determined saint and the greedy relatives became the turning point for Vakhtangov's interpretation.

Vakhtangov's clear disgust for the bourgeoisie had been present in his other projects, particularly in his creations as an actor for characters such as Fraser in *The Flood* and Takleton in *Cricket on the Hearth*. In *The Miracle of St. Anthony* he was able to infuse his actors with his own viewpoint, supported by the attitudes of the post-revolution society which surrounded them. Vakhtangov wanted his productions to reflect the point of view of the new revolutionary audience, allowing domestic psychological comedy to transform into tragic farce. "The actors must not only reveal these Achilles and Gustaves in a psychologically truthful manner: They must also clearly define their common fundamental class features" (Khersonsky 226).[10]

These "Achilles and Gustaves" refers to the greedy heirs who are alarmed by St. Anthony and see him not as a benevolent saint but as someone who has come to rob them of their newly found fortune. From the curate to the doctor to the police, they fight him with everything in their power, while the kindly old maid, who stands to lose her modest bequest, shows only joy at the prospect of her mistress's return to the world of the living.

To facilitate the expression of this attitude and to emphasize the contrasts between the characters, Vakhtangov guided his actors to develop a physical characterization for their roles which reflected an inner psychological state. He required Zavadskii as St. Anthony and Kotlubai as Virginia, the maid, to work toward natural movement expressing simplicity, sincerity and humanity. This was in sharp contrast with the grotesque approach to the physicality of the bourgeois characters, which approached caricature.

Vakhtangov was inspired by the political lithographs of the French artist, Honoré Daumier in whose satirical works Vakhtangov found a graphic panorama of bourgeois psychology which he shared with his actors. It was the task of the actors to find ways to physically satirize their characters while remaining firmly grounded in a psychological analysis of the roles as they had been taught by Stanislavsky through Vakhtangov.

In his discussion of characterization in *St. Anthony*, Simonov adamantly insists that the acting was realistic despite the grotesque style of each actor's physicality. True to his training, Vakhtangov "demanded of us a complete belief in the given circumstances of the play" in order to avoid a distortion of the "scenic truth." At the same time, however, "it was necessary to avoid formlessness, looseness, unrhythmicality of actions" (91).

A balance of reality and fantasy came to be the hallmark of Vakhtangov's work as a director. In the case of this production, one method by which he achieved balance was in contrasting internal psychology and external physicality in order to produce satire. "The satirical and ridiculous came about as a result of the disparity in manner in which well-bred people would be expected to behave and the way they actually do behave" (Simonov 92).

Shchukin, for example, in the role of the curate, was able to physically create the image of a "life-loving, healthy glutton who indulged in all the joys of living" (Simonov 95). In addition to building an outward appearance, Shchukin also devised a voice and manner of speech which organically supported his creation.

> He talked with a high-pitched, thin, tenor voice, in a sing-song tone. Beginning the speech with a melodic, mellifluous voice, Shchukin gradually reinforced the sound, imperceptibly changing it into the church recitative, and then went into singing. That reinforcing of his voice was done indiscernibly; we would suddenly notice that at the end of a phrase the *curé* was not talking but singing (Simonov 96).

Just as a caricaturist will emphasize and underscore an insignificant but distinctive physical characteristic in order to satirize, Shchukin molded his role on his psychological understanding of the character blended with a subtle enhancement of reality which expressed outwardly the inner man. In a similar manner, each of the actors playing the bourgeois roles found some telling trait to assist in the expression of character.

In this second version of *The Miracle of St. Anthony*, Vakhtangov sought to draw out the rhythm and plasticity of the actors' performances. He believed that an expression of the inner life of the character must be consciously guided with precision and mastery and not allowed to simply occur spontaneously. Only then would the actors have the freedom to improvise with gesture, intonation and movement (Khersonsky 226). The end result, while it was strongly related to the work of Meyerhold, was in itself much deeper in its expression.

While Meyerhold, in his 1906 production *of The Miracle of St. Anthony*, had used masks to indicate the soulless nature of the bourgeoisie, Vakhtangov chose to guide his actors towards the use of Stanislavsky's "system" to find instead the distortions of the human soul which radiated from these characters. This search led to the discovery that these bourgeois philistines wanted only two things: to preserve their fortunes and to hide their true selves from each other. By emphasizing the characters' desire to conceal their shallowness from each other, the true nature of their impoverished souls became sharply defined and clearly revealed to the audience, particularly when juxtaposed with the humanity of St. Anthony and Virginia. It also gave the actors a concrete through-line of action to pursue, something Stanislavsky's "system" demands.

The Miracle of St. Anthony was a tremendous success for the Third Studio of the Moscow Art Theatre. It spoke to the post-revolutionary Russian audience in terms they could appreciate, moving the emphasis of the play away from the religious realm and into the world of social satire. Of course, in 1921 the bourgeoisie was an easy target; but this production nevertheless was a brilliant example of Vakhtangov's ability to use the best features of old methods to enhance the renewed theatricality he hoped to bring to the Russian stage.

While working on *The Miracle of St. Anthony*, Vakhtangov was also directing Strindberg's *Erik XIV* at the First Studio. It is therefore not surprising that there are many similarities between the two productions. Like *St. Anthony*, *Erik XIV* was an exercise in contrast; but while *St. Anthony* expressed the contrast between simple hearts and greedy heartlessness, *Erik XIV* juxtaposed the world of the living with the world of the dead. Once again Vakhtangov used the goodness of common people in contrast with the decadent and pathological nature of life in the upper class. He also saw in the play not just a historical king of Sweden, but an image symbolic of the rights of a monarch. For Vakhtangov, the overriding theme could best be expressed in the following way:

The power of a king sooner or later is destroyed due to the strength of its inner contradiction.... [For Erik it was] a conflict between the wish to become a democratic and beneficent "father of the people" and the necessity to depend for support on feudal aristocracy and subordinate his actions to its interests.... Erik cannot ultimately resolve his conflicts either with the aristocracy or with the people (peasants,) or with the people close to him. The destruction of such an Erik-the-man on the throne, was inevitable. For Erik the throne became a scaffold. The destruction of such a king, who had dared to be a man, was shown not in realistic, persuasive concrete-historic terms, but in an abstract, expressionistic treatment (Khersonsky 228–233).[11]

This expressionistic treatment of the theme was most striking in the visual aspects of the production.

As in *The Miracle of St. Anthony*, in *Erik XIV* the simple people, who personified the world of the living, were drawn in a realistic way in order to contrast most strikingly with the courtiers, who inhabited the world of the dead. Erik and his courtiers wore mask-like make-up and highly stylized costumes which approached the allegorical. This approach even carried over into the movement of the actors, with Birman as the queen-mother, for example, floating about the castle hall like a bat and courtiers who stood as still as the stones that surrounded them (Zorgraf 96–97).

Erik XIV was a pivotal production for the First Studio, marking a major step away from the traditions of the Moscow Art Theatre. It was more closely related to the work Vakhtangov was doing in his other studios at the time than to anything the First Studio had produced previously. For Vakhtangov it led directly to his next important project, *The Dybbuk*.

In 1918 a group of young Jewish amateur actors approached Stanislavsky with the project of founding a new Jewish theatre. During the Tsarist era many edicts restricting the movements of Jews had been enacted which were repealed with the Revolution. Consequently an influx of Jews from Eastern Europe had moved into the interior of Russia. For the first time in many years theatre specifically for Jewish audiences could be produced and the founders of the Habima Theatre wanted to produce it.

One of the first issues the Habima Theatre had to resolve was the selection of a language for performances. Although many of the new immigrants spoke Yiddish, they knew they would be performing for an audience that included many people who had already assimilated Russian culture and spoke primarily Russian. As the language of performance, The Habima Players chose to perform in modern Hebrew, which was being revived in Palestine from ancient Biblical sources and which was unknown to both segments of their audience. It was also unknown to Vakhtangov, the teacher/director Stanislavsky recommended to the group.

At this time Vakhtangov was already overextended in his directorial commitments. He was involved in productions or lessons at the First Studio, Second Studio, Mansurovsky Studio, People's Theatre, Proletkult and Moscow Art Theatre. He could not, however, resist the opportunity to work with these enthusiastic and energetic young people. He began with lessons in Stanislavsky's "system" followed by a series of short plays and concert performances. At this time Vakhtangov was attempting to learn Hebrew but discontinued his studies when he decided that the essence of understanding this language was contained in hand gestures. He believed that gestures used by Hebrew speakers "reveal the speaker's hidden feelings about his subjects, his words, even the persons that he is addressing, but are not mimed images" (Gordon 92). Since few of the spectators at the Habima's performances would be able to understand Hebrew, Vakhtangov believed it was better if he was not fluent either. In that way he could concentrate on clear communication through movement and gesture, particularly through the use of the actors' hands, instead of relying on a knowledge of the spoken dialogue.

The Dybbuk, a play of mysticism and legend, was a perfect vehicle for Vakhtangov's experiments in non-verbal communication. It was also another opportunity for him to move away from realism and toward the theatricality he sought.

The story of *The Dybbuk* is based both on Jewish folklore and a case of demon possession that occurred in an isolated Russian village. The play was written by the Jewish folklorist and historian Solomon Rappoport, under the pen-name S. Ansky. It was originally written in Russian but was then translated into Hebrew and Yiddish. The playwright's ethnographic research provided a rich backdrop for the production which assisted Vakhtangov in his search for the proper form.

The rehearsal process for the production included many hours of exploration during which Vakhtangov would gather the actors on the stage and, with nothing but candlelight for illumination, listen to the retelling of old Jewish legends. In this way he hoped to find the heart of the play. He heavily edited the script and, motivated by a desire to exclude all extraneous elements, condensed four acts into three in his search for the essential truths of the play.

Once again Vakhtangov saw an opportunity to use a production as a vehicle through which to address post-revolutionary Russia. Since the time of the Revolution, Vakhtangov had perceived the world as divided into two factions: the old world of those who resisted change, and the new world of those striving towards a better future. As he explored the theme of *The Dybbuk* he returned to the vision of contrasting worlds he had already explored in *The Miracle of St. Anthony* and *Erik XIV*. This time, however, the mysticism of the piece gave a different flavor to the contrast than he had elaborated in the previous productions. In this case the theme, despite the ethnicity of the production, was humanity in general rather than the ills of a particular society. Khersonsky describes Vakhtangov's approach in the following way:

> The line of demarcation goes between two worlds—not between heaven, (mystical notions or even nothing more than a poetic abstraction) and the earth and not simply between the world of the poor and the rich, but between living, with real human feelings and destinies, on one hand, and the cursed world of the past with its way of life, religion, laws on the other. A person cannot live, cannot keep his wonderful living soul in the world of oppression, abnormality and fear (246).[12]

It was indeed a world of oppression, abnormality and fear that Vakhtangov created for the setting of *The Dybbuk*. He was greatly aided in the task of creating such a world by the work of his stage designer, Nathan Altman. According to historian Anatoly Smeliansky, when Altman showed his sketches to Vakhtangov, the director was stunned by the images he saw. Altman had especially captured the essence of Vakhtangov's vision in his drawings of the people. In the sketches, the characters were bent, shriveled people who resembled trees growing on dry soil. Photographs of the production clearly show the people of the old world in postures which are barely human, crouched and nearly shapeless, with hands sharply defined against their dark clothing.

As he had done in *The Miracle of St. Anthony*, Vakhtangov rendered the production in black and white with dramatic use of light. As in *Rosmersholm*, he emphasized the actors' hands; and as in *Erik XIV*, he tightly controlled the actors' movements in ways that approached choreography. What resulted was a production that relied heavily on visual and musical means to transcend the language barrier and move the audience emotionally.

A chorus of beggars danced frenetically, their movements building and growing in intensity until they approached a physical embodiment of madness. This "bacchical ecstasy" conveyed the "mythological symbolism" of the piece while Vakhtangov's adherence to Wagnerian ideals "succeeded in transcending the meaning of the play far beyond his own conception" (Orani 475). One again Vakhtangov had placed on the stage a production which reflected for the new Russian society the revolutionary social struggle, embodying the fight for freedom from the old world. The conflicts in this play not only addressed class struggle and confrontation, but encompassed the ideals of self-liberation as well.

Following the success of *The Dybbuk* at the Habima Theatre, Vakhtangov embarked on what would be his last and perhaps most enduring project, Carlo Gozzi's *Princess Turandot*. In contrast to his previous productions, in *Princess Turandot* Vakhtangov, "does not develop a significant social theme, but concentrates his attention on finding the principles of a new theatre and its means of expression, on a quest for a form of romantic representation" (Zorgraf 124).[13]

Early in 1920, a student suggested Schiller's poetic version of *Princess Turandot* for consideration by the Studio. Vakhtangov was intrigued with the idea and entrusted it to Zavadskii and Kotlubai, his leading students, for early explorations of the project. Later Vakhtangov took control of the rehearsals.

At first the studio members tried to create a fairy-tale atmosphere for the production. Despite their efforts, the work did not please Vakhtangov, who felt it did not have a well-focused purpose and would be inappropriate for modern audiences. He did not believe a detailed reconstruction of China in the style of Reinhardt would be effective, nor would a psychological approach to the love story be of interest. For a time the project was dropped. Vakhtangov did not stop thinking about the play, however, and eventually proposed to his studio that they consider Carlo Gozzi's *Princess Turandot* instead. He believed that Schiller's telling of the story was overly sentimental and would not appeal to the modern audience while Gozzi's version emphasized the fantastic nature of the tale and was much better suited to both his actors and his audience (Khersonsky 276).

Vakhtangov's vision was to re-create the spontaneous, unsophisticated performances of Commedia dell'arte as a framework for the piece. He hoped to bring to the stage the bright colors, humor and zest for living characteristic of Italian street theatre, while allowing the actors to work within what he considered the most important moment of creativity, improvisation.

Vakhtangov also believed it was necessary to involve the audience in this production. He "widened the actor's 'center of attention' during the rehearsals of *Turandot*. He moved the 'fourth wall' over the footlights to the last row of the orchestra and gallery" (Simonov 163). There were moments in the play when the action moved into the auditorium, and at that time the house lights were lit, signifying to the spectators that this was their opportunity to become even more closely involved in the creative process and interact with the actors more directly. No attempts were made to hide any aspect of the performance from the audience. All "secrets of the performing art" were joyfully revealed (Simonov 163).

In his approach to this production, Vakhtangov wanted to emphasize the actor above all else. Scenic considerations were secondary to acting skill. The performance style was presentational and direct, reveling in its own theatricality. While working with his actors at this time, Vakhtangov remained true to Stanislavsky's "system," adapting it to meet the needs of this particular project. He had long felt that it was essential to approach each play on its own terms, finding the uniquely correct form and method for each piece.

For *Turandot* Vakhtangov added a condition to Stanislavsky's "Magic If" appropriate to his conception of the production. Because he wanted the actors to approach their roles as if they were members of a Commedia troupe presenting the play of *Princess Turandot*, he included that condition from the very beginning of their character work. For this production he formulated the "Magic If" in the following terms: "If you were an actor of the People's Theater, creating the role of Kalaf, how would you behave in the given circumstances of the play?" (Simonov 163). In this way he was adapting Stanislavsky's principles in order to help the actors find the additional layer of required characterization for their interpretations.

Finally, after many difficult months of preparation, the production was nearly ready to be shown. Vakhtangov's health was failing and everyone involved in the production was well aware that it could indeed be their beloved teacher's last project. During long nights of rehearsals, Studio members became increasingly aware that their leader's time with them was limited. There was, nevertheless, a feeling of celebration in the work. While the students hid their fear, the teacher hid his tremendous physical pain, each out of love and concern for the other. As Simonov, who was a member of the studio, describes the final rehearsal period, "We were possessed with one desire: to do our very best with all our ability and fulfill all of Vakhtangov's demands. Perhaps thus we might ease his suffering" (166). When Vakhtangov was taken home following a late rehearsal on February 23, 1922, it would prove to be the last time he saw the inside of his theatre. For many years the sixth row seat from which he had worked was reserved in his memory.

His illness did not prevent Vakhtangov from continuing to work on the production, however. In the days that followed, his actors and assistants came to his home to talk over difficulties and work out solutions. Four days after Vakhtangov's last rehearsal in the theatre, the production was shown to invited guests from the Moscow Art Theatre, its studios and the Habima Theatre. Simonov relates the excitement that flowed through the dressing rooms when word reached the actors that Nemirovich-Danchenko and Stanislavsky had arrived. What followed was a performance that marked the climax of Vakhtangov's brilliant career.

In order to establish immediately the flavor of the production, Vakhtangov opened the performance with the "parade." To the accompaniment of an orchestra which included such sophisticated instruments as the comb and tissue paper, the actors, dressed in formal evening attire, wrapped themselves in colorful lengths of fabric and applied make-up to their faces in full view of the audience. Within a few minutes all were ready and Truffaldino, one of the four traditional Commedia dell'arte characters at the heart of the production, announced, "We are ready," and the company sang their opening song:

> Here we begin
> With our simple song.
> In five minutes China
> Will become our rough platform.
>
> All of us in this tale
> Are your servants and your friends
> Among us four "masks"
> It is I, I, I, and I.

Then the actors formed a line and, coiling around the stage, danced off while the stage crew, in full view and wearing coveralls, changed the set in time to the music.

> They let down the ropes with colorful weights. Three very wide drop-curtains are hung on the sticks. On the curtains there is an appliqué picturing a Chinese town. The stage servants pull the cloth-made scenery, which is simultaneously flying up, and with fairy-like speed, we find ourselves in Peking. There is no doubt that we are in Peking because we are so informed by very large letters reading PEKING on the curtain (Simonov 172).

And thus the light-hearted, presentational tone for the production was established. This tone was carried into the properties and costuming as well. Timur's beard, for example, was a towel, the old wise men wore shoelace moustaches and headdresses made of fruit baskets. Chan's crown was a lampshade and his royal scepter was a tennis racket. The four Commedia "masks" painted large, round, black eyeglasses on their faces. Every element of the production was coordinated in such a way as to support the overall mood of child-like innocence and celebration.

Even before the performance ended, *Princess Turandot* was a tremendous success for the Third Studio. During intermission Stanislavsky rushed from the theatre to Vakhtangov's home to congratulate the director on his stunning success. On his return, the play was resumed and as it progressed the excitement in the theatre continued to build. The last act was enthusiastically performed and received with "roars of laughter and storms of applause." At the conclusion of the performance, as the actors removed their make-up and costumes on the stage, the line between actors and audience completely disappeared. The triumphant performers and the exuberant audience members remained in the auditorium, reliving the joyful moments of the play while the orchestra played the musical numbers from *Turandot* again and Vakhtangov's friends, comrades in the theatre and students composed a telegram of gratitude and love to their dear colleague (Simonov 190).

The production of *Princess Turandot* exceeded all expectations, and with it Vakhtangov proved conclusively that Stanislavsky's "system" had much wider applications than had previously been believed. With this production Vakhtangov demonstrated unequivocally that the "system" and theatricality were not mutually exclusive and he won a decisive battle in his war against "...naturalism, facelessness, and grayishness in art" (Simonov 199).

For the members of the Third Studio, the triumph of *Turandot* was bitter-sweet. While they celebrated their success, they also mourned what they knew they would soon lose. Vakhtangov was on his deathbed and there was no longer any hope for recovery. He lingered for three months until, on May 29, Nadezhda Mikhailovna telephoned the studio and urged the members to come quickly to Vakhtangov's side. At 9:55 pm., Evgenii Bogrationovich died, surrounded by a loving circle of his students and colleagues.[14]

Vakhtangov's legacy to the world of theatre is two-fold. First he was a dedicated teacher, sharing the ideas of Stanislavsky along with his own adaptations and experimentations, with his contemporaries as well as with a new generation of actors. Second, he was a director of major stature, embracing the best techniques of the past and synthesizing them with a vision of the future in order to set the tone for a new era in the theatre. In his eulogy for Vakhtangov, Nemirovich-Danchenko said:

> In his creative endeavor Vakhtangov did not strive to divorce himself from the M.A.T., though he did divorce himself from its bad traditions. What were these traditions? The naturalism of which the M.A.T. wants to rid itself... And it was of this drab, tedious naturalism that Vakhtangov rid himself with such spontaneous finality (Gorchakov qtd. in Orani, 480).

Of course the death of Vakhtangov left a tremendous void in the Third Studio, but it was not the end of that organization. The Studio did, however, enter a period marked by diminished artistic growth as well as a crisis of leadership. Vakhtangov had required an active search for the unique form and style appropriate to each piece. Without his guidance, it was difficult for the Studio to avoid merely repeating past successes, superimposing onto new projects the ideas which had worked in previous productions.

In the 1922–23 season only one new production was staged: Ostrovsky's *Truth is Good but Happiness is Better (Правда хорошо—а счастье лучше*) directed by Boris Zakhava. The production repeated many of the theatrical devices used in *The Miracle of St. Anthony*, but the grotesque approach to characterization did not harmonize with the realistic nature of Ostrovsky's comedy. The production was a failure. The following year the Studio staged *The Wedding* (*Женитьба*) by Gogol, with Yuri Zavadskii serving as director. Once again the concept for the production imitated Vakhtangov's work in the production of other plays which, in this case gave the impression of "formalistic pretense" (Simonov in *Vakhtangov 20 Years* 28).[15]

While the Third Studio was floundering without a sense of direction, the Moscow Art Theatre was also in difficulty. Shortly after Vakhtangov's death the core of the Art Theatre went to America on tour for more than two years. During this time the members of all of the Studios filled the gaps left in the parent troupe. There was increasing unrest throughout the organization, and Nemirovich-Danchenko attempted to bring order by inviting various Studio groups to join the Art Theatre proper.

At one time Nemirovich proposed that the Third Studio be absorbed into the Moscow Art Theatre and cease to exist as a separate entity. The members of the Studio answered this proposal with the condition that they be permitted to preserve the productions of Vakhtangov on the small stage of the Moscow Art.

Another proposal was offered by the Studio in a letter to Stanislavsky. The Studio members urged Stanislavsky to run their Studio together with Vsevelod Meyerhold. This was a return to an earlier suggestion of Vakhtangov's designed to "rescue Stanislavski (*sic*) from the deadening clutches of the Art Theatre" (Benedetti 266). None of these proposals was ever successfully negotiated, and as a result some members of the Third Studio joined the Second Studio and thereby became members of the Moscow Art Theatre, while the remaining members established an independent theatre bearing Vakhtangov's name. This independent theatre still exists today in its home on the Moscow Arbat.

Evgenii Vakhtangov's work had a great impact on many actors and directors who followed him. He set the tone for a new era in Russian theatre in response to the fledgling Soviet society. His work with Stanislavsky's "system" was crucial in terms of testing its practical applications for actors. Mel Gordon summarizes Vakhtangov's contributions in the following way:

> How much Vakhtangov radically altered or transformed the Stanislavsky System's basic teachings is debatable. Nothing that Stanislavsky or Sulerzhitskii (*sic*) taught was rejected by their pupil. But by the early

twenties, Vakhtangov's acting theories and methods appeared heretical to Stanislavsky's most devoted followers. Vakhtangov, it seemed, with his emphasis on the actor's physicality and the grotesque qualities in his productions, often at the expense of the play's logic, had gone the way of Meyerhold. Only after *Turandot's* success and Vakhtangov's death did Stanislavsky realize that many of Vakhtangov's reformulations were valuable additions to his System training (101).

As time passed, Stanislavsky himself did not hesitate to draw on the "reformulations" and "valuable additions" that were developed in the Third Studio by his most talented student and disciple.

Evgenii Vakhtangov

Scene from *The Miracle of St. Anthony*, 1921

The Third Studio

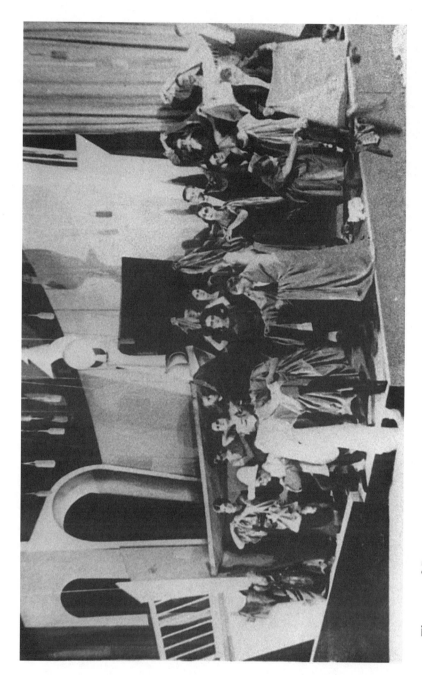

The cast of *Princess Turandot* donning costumes and make-up onstage during the opening prologue

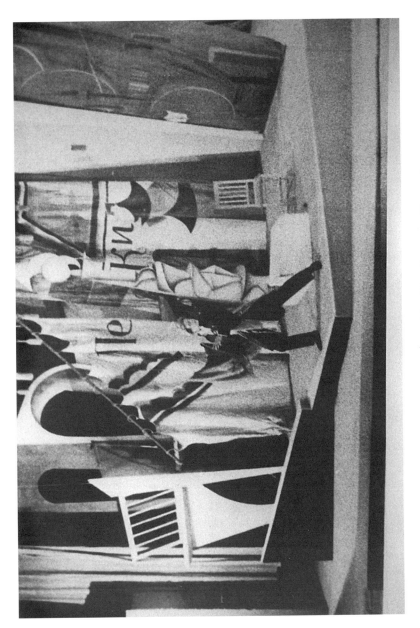

The Stylized "Street in Peking" in *Princess Turandot*

A traditional Commedia "mask" with "Kalaf" in *Princess Turandot*

CONCLUSION

The studios of the Moscow Art Theatre played an invaluable role in the course of Western theatre during the twentieth century. Each studio was unique and made its own contributions to the changing face of theatre but, when examined as a group a through-line of experimentation and discovery can be discerned. Each in its own way had a profound effect on both theatrical practice and actor training which is still felt today, nearly a century after the founding of the Studio on Povarskaya. The studio setting offered the freedom to try new approaches to staging, to explore new dramatic literature, and most importantly, it gave Konstantin Stanislavsky the opportunity to work in an atmosphere conducive to the practical application of his emerging "grammar" of actor training.

When examining the work of the studios it is important to recognize them as points on a continuum of development, each of which added to the common threads which ran throughout. Each studio began with high hopes and shining visions of the future. The members believed they were embarking on a great quest which would result in the revitalization of a stagnating theatrical scene. Similarly, each studio found that with time their dreams began to fade, their enthusiasm waned and the end result was disillusionment and distrust. In many ways, each of the three major studios was like a child to Stanislavsky and, like real children, each one was destined to rebel against its parent while searching for its own maturity. It was Stanislavsky's great sorrow that his children, "daughters" to his "Lear," could not stay close to him.

Throughout his entire life, at the heart of Stanislavsky's work was a search for truth on the stage. When the Moscow Art Theatre was formed, he believed that truth could be found in attention to detail and a carefully researched and faithfully produced *mise-en-scene*. While this approach worked for a time, he soon came to realize that he had not yet found the truth he sought. His continuing search led him to the plays of the Symbolist writers in whose work he hoped to find a new, more truthful aesthetic. This became the nucleus of the work at the Studio on Povarskaya.

It was in conjunction with the Studio on Povarskaya that the term "studio" was defined for the Moscow Art Theatre. Originally it was Meyerhold who proposed the word, intended to imply an institution somewhere between a professional theatre and a school. It is important to remember that the Moscow Art Theatre always operated a school for the training of actors and other theatre artists, but the studios were a separate entity. The Studio on Povarskaya was inhabited by young people who had already received a standard theatrical school training but were not yet attached to a professional company. The original plan for the studio was to create such a company which could produce plays from the traditional repertoire while experimenting with ways to bring the new dramatic literature to the stage.

Financially, the Studio on Povarskaya was a failure. Its productions were never performed for the public and it closed within a few months of its beginning. From an artistic standpoint, however, it knew some success. The productions themselves failed, but it is often in failure that learning occurs, and that was the real contribution of this studio. Among the lessons learned at the Studio on Povarskaya was the incompatibility between a theatre where actors are the core and one where the director takes first priority. This conflict was one of the fundamental differences between Stanislavsky and Meyerhold which frequently surfaced in their dealings with each other.

Another lesson learned was that the new plays needed a new type of setting. The rehearsals that offered such promise in Pushkino were performed in front of a plain canvas, but that promise disappeared when the actors were placed in front of a backdrop that overwhelmed them. Similarly, the music composed for the Studio productions was thrilling in itself, but did not unite with the work of the other artists.

Had the difficulties of the 1905 revolution not interfered with the operation of the Studio on Povarskaya, it is possible these lessons would have resulted in further, more successful work, but financially it was impossible to keep the project alive. The most profoundly positive result of the Studio on Povarskaya, however, was not lost in the turmoil of social upheaval. As a direct result of the work at the Studio on Povarskaya, Stanislavsky became convinced that what was needed most was not new plays but new actors and it became his mission to find a way to train those actors so that they would have the tools necessary to bring about a true revolution in the theatre.

Over the next seven years, Stanislavsky continued to work on his ideas for actor training, searching for the keys to the actor's art which would unlock the doors which separated him from the truthful expression he believed was possible on the stage. He tried to analyze the performances of the great actors he had seen and to examine in depth his own past and present work. He filled his notebooks with his thoughts about communicating emotion, accessing an actor's feelings, objectives, characterization and self-analysis. He worked on methods for teaching relaxation, breath control, mental concentration and the release of bodily tension, all of which are now considered the basic building blocks of any good actor training program. He was searching for a way to help actors recreate emotions with each performance, rather than mechanically reproducing what had been discovered during the rehearsal process, the method he believed had been most commonly used both by his colleagues and himself. He hoped to find the balance between total identification with a character, which could become pathological, and the ability to create a lived experience on the stage. Over the course of these years he looked for and found other people who shared his hopes for a new approach to acting, the most influential of which was Leopold Sulerzhitskii.

Sulerzhitskii brought to Stanislavsky's work his energy, enthusiasm and humanism. His own personal philosophy permeated everything he did and spread to those around him. His belief that a good actor must also be a good person and, conversely, that good actor training was good person training, brought an important ethical element to Stanislavsky's emerging "system" and the studios in which it was implemented.

When the two men formed the First Studio of the Moscow Art Theatre in 1912, they had already tried to impose their ideas on the experienced actors of the Moscow Art with little or no success. Stanislavsky and Sulerzhitskii had come to realize that what was needed were young people who were not novices in the theatre arts, but were still flexible enough to remain open-minded about a new approach. Their youthful idealism, furthermore, made them receptive to Suler's ethical and spiritual beliefs. The enthusiastic members of the new Studio eagerly entered into the experiments, confident that they could work together to refine Stanislavsky's "system" and find a way to transform the theory into practice.

One important step taken by the Studio was to move away from Naturalism and toward the "Spiritual Realism" Stanislavsky and Suler were searching for as a means of going beyond mere physical imitation and toward the inner truth they believed was just beyond their grasp. This step was facilitated by the limited financial resources available to the Studio. While it is tempting to say that the move away from elaborately mounted productions to a more symbolic or minimal setting was instigated by the careful consideration of aesthetics, in reality it was more of a serendipitous happenstance precipitated by practical necessities, a situation which was common to all of the major studios. The resulting simple stagings were effective, nevertheless, and certainly focused attention on the craft of the actors and away from questions of design. The nature of the studio facilities was such that the line between the actors and the audience was often and inevitably blurred and the resultant acting style, in which the slightest gesture or the most subtle change of expression could be clearly seen by everyone, created a heightened sense of intimacy in comparison to the large auditorium of the Moscow Art Theatre. This understated style of acting, supported by intense psychological character work, became the hallmark, not only of the studios, but of a whole generation of actors throughout Europe and the United States who followed in their footsteps.

Another important function of the First Studio was performed by Evgenii Vakhtangov and Mikhail Chekhov. Not only did these two men embrace the "system," they cared about it enough to question it. Vakhtangov was one of the very first to teach the "system" to his students and relied on it to give his actors the foundation they needed in order to discover the truth within the grotesque characterizations he required them to create; not Suler and Stanislavsky's "Spiritual Realism" but his own "Fantastic Realism."

For his part, Mikhail Chekhov took the basic ideas of the "system" and expanded them to enable the actor to fully engage both his own experienced emotions and the full range of his imagination as well and did not limit himself to working only from the psychological to the physical, but when necessary used the physical to find the psychological. Not only did Chekhov become one of the finest character actors of the twentieth century, when he left Russia he spread his version of the "system" throughout Europe and the United States. Both of these men refined and expanded Stanislavsky's "system" in ways that Konstantin Sergeevich appreciated and approved, despite their frequent disagreements over form.

The artistic life of Stanislavsky and his studios was not always a comfortable one and can be likened to a swinging pendulum, constantly in motion, forever moving between extremes. When, after the death of Suler, Vakhtangov and Chekhov tried to move the First Studio away from the subtle playing of its early years toward a broader, more theatrical style reminiscent of Meyerhold's work at the Studio on Povarskaya, Stanislavsky was skeptical and disapproving. A few years later, however, he realized that with the Third Studio's production of *Princess Turandot*, Vakhtangov had successfully created a bridge between the two styles of performance, proving that the "system" had much wider applications than had previously been believed. He also demonstrated unequivocally that the "system" and theatricality need not be mutually exclusive.

For a time the Second Studio seemed to be the one which would remain true to Stanislavsky's vision, accepting it without question, as if it were gospel. The members of the Second Studio wanted nothing more than to study with the master and absorb everything he could give them.

During their first years they produced plays in the style of the Moscow Art Theatre, successfully creating on the stage characters who were in many ways similar to themselves. Then, with the advent of the Revolution, the members of the Second Studio took their performances of classic plays to the masses, performing in factories and workers' clubs in response to both Lunacharsky's vision and their own political beliefs. While this period proved to be good training for the Studio members, it did not produce any innovative or experimental work like that produced in the other studios. Even though the Second Studio, when left to its own devices in 1922, attempted to create something new with *The Robbers*, they did not have the ability to break the mold into which they had been formed. When the re-organization came, were fairly easily assimilated into the parent Moscow Art Theatre organization.

The greatest contribution made by the Second Studio was the way its members brought their training in the "system" into the Moscow Art Theatre proper. With the production of *The Days of the Turbins* the second generation proved itself worthy of inclusion in the internationally renowned company of the Moscow Art Theatre. Then, with *Armoured Train 14–69* they worked together with the members of the first generation, permeating the company with their methods and guiding the veterans toward the actual implementation of what had long been the offical, in theory if not in practice, working method of the Moscow Art Theatre. In this manner the second generation was not only the one that "sovietized" the Moscow Art Theatre, they were the one that, to a large degree, "systemized" it as well, finally making it in reality the wellspring of Stanislavsky's "system" that outsiders had long believed it to be.

The irony of the Second Studio is that it never lived up to its promise or its dreams. The members of the second generation believed that the new, post-Revolutionary order would bring them an artistic freedom previously unknown in Russia. They supported the changes being made in their country and wanted to do their part to bring about the new Russia. The reality was that whenever they conceded an artistic point to the government officials who questioned their work, it was in the hope that the next compromise would be in their favor but this was not the case. Beginning with *The Days of the Turbins* and continuing for the rest of their careers, the members of the second generation found themselves constantly marking time or moving backwards, never progressing forward.

A further irony is that the Second Studio, the one that appeared to be the closest to Stanislavsky and his teaching, the one he referred to as his "Cordelia," was also the one that was farthest away from him. The evolution of the Second Studio was toward the Revolution, but Stanislavsky was not prepared for the new order and did not understand the protocols of Soviet life. Then, during his two years abroad with the touring company, Stanislavsky completely lost touch with the members of the Second Studio to the point of barely knowing who they were. As the 1920's ended and the 1930's began, Stanislavsy turned away from the second generation and turned his attention toward the next group of students, hoping yet again to find the truth which he had always sought.

Ultimately, the importance of the studios in relation to the work of Stanislavsky on his "system" is the real focus of this book. I hope that, by pursuing this study I have eliminated some major misconceptions which are widely accepted, at least outside of Russia. First, the idea that the "system" came from the Moscow Art Theatre itself is untrue. In reality, the members of the Moscow Art Theatre strongly resisted the adoption of the "system" as a method of approaching a role and it was not until the mid-1920's, after word of Stanislavsky's work had already sparked great excitement outside of Russia, that the "system" became accepted in its supposed birthplace.

Second, the image of the "system" as a monolithic entity which sprang fullblown from the pen of Stanislavsky is also a misconception. The "system" was a living, breathing, changing, growing organism which was never fully complete. Stanislavsky continued to work on it: always searching for a way to put truth on the stage, always trying new ideas and experimenting until the end of his life. And finally, it is important to realize that the "system" was not the work of just one man but a wide-ranging project which benefitted from the experiments and adaptations of many other talented and dedicated theatre professionals.

A century has passed since that legendary conversation at the Slavianskii Bazaar which marks the birth of the Moscow Art Theatre. Over the years the Moscow Art Theatre came to represent the best of Russian culture, especially for foreigners. As a result of the Revolution and the years of silence which followed, the image of the Moscow Art Theatre and the "System of Actor Training" that it supposedly developed bears little resemblence to the truth. Stanislavsky would hate that. I hope this book has to some small degree rectified that situation.

ENDNOTES

Introduction

[1]There were two separate Opera studios which should not be confused. In July, 1935, Stanislavsky created a new Opera-Dramatic Studio which was intended to be a place for creative experiment, especially in relation to his exploration of the Method of Physical Action which occupied him during the last years of his life. This studio falls well outside of the chronological delimitation. Furthermore, due to Stanislavsky's failing health, the work he began there was never fully developed. This studio, which should not be confused with the original Opera Studio, is also excluded from the book.

[2]See Chapter 3

Chapter One

[1]Сам Художественный театр с его натуральностью игры не есть, конечно, последнее слово и не думает останавливаться на точке замерзания: «молодой» театр наряду с его родоначальником должен продолжать дело и итти далее (Статьи, Речи, Беседы, Письма 175).

[2]While it seems incredible that such a large number of plays could be produced in this period of time, Hoover indicates that this was indeed the case. She writes, "Of course the great number of plays staged—often a new one every other day—mainly demonstrated the ruthless frequency with which one new bill must follow the other in a repertory system" (22).

[3]There is a possible confusion in the sources concerning the second season. While Rudnitsky places the company in Tbilisi, Marjorie Hoover places it in Tiflis. In reality, these are both the same city. Tiflis is the pre-Soviet name and Tbilisi the name which was adopted following the revolution.

[4]...самым честным, самым уважаемым, самым культурным, самым авторитетным человеком.

[5]While one can assume Prince Sherbatov was a friend and colleague of Stanislavsky, I have been unable to find mention of him in the literature as yet. In private conversation, Smeliansky has asserted that this was a joke on the part of Stanislavsky, since Sherbatov was one of the many minor noblemen with whom Stanislavsky was acquainted and who, as was common practice at that time, was probably a supporter of the Moscow Art Theatre but was not associated with it in any artistic or creative way.

[6]Подходит единственный человек—это Всевелод Мейерхольд, но он в ссоре с театром. Я все—таки пошлю ему телеграмму с предложением (68-69).

[7]Povarskaya Street has also been known as Vorovsky Street.

[8]В настоящее время пробуждения общественных сил в стране театр не может и не имеет права служить только чистому искусству—он должен отзыватся на общественные настроения, выяснать их публике, быть учителем обществаю И, не забывая о своем высоком общественном призвании, «молодой» театр должен в то же время стремиться к осусшесвлению главной свой задачи—обновлению драматического исполнения (Статьи, Речи, Беседы, Письма 175).

[9] Репетиции Мейерхольда были необычайно увлекательны и смотреть их было не менее интересно и полезно, чем участвовать в пьесе (32).

[10]Игрена, Беланжера, Тентажиль передавали свои чуства холодным звуком, но в нем ощущалось затаенное волнение, и вся эмоция ложилась на паузу, которая являлась следствием наивысшего напряжения чусвств. Там, где в натуралистическом исполнении был бы выкрик, он заменялся неожиданным интенсивным молчанием (Встречи с Мейерхольдом 33).

[11] дал мне много радости (344)

[12] произвел фурор (344)

[13] «Комедия любви» прошла слабо, но я, кажется, понял секрет и смогу подать хороший совет. Главное же в том, что вчера стало ясно: есть труппа, или, вернее, хороший материал для нее. Этот вопрос мучил меня все лето, и вчера я успокоился. Вчера пессимисты стали верить в успех и признали первую победу студии (344).

[14] Я не иду против общего мнения, но прошу только взвесить все поставленные вопросы и оценить их, что важнее сейчас: всячески подгонять художественную работу или зан-яться полом (Попов 340).

[15] На сцене полумрак, видны только силуэты людей, плоскостная декорация, без кулис, задник повешен почти у рампы. Это ново, по-новому со сцены доносится ритмическая реч актеров. Медленно развивается действие, кажется, время остановилось. Вдруг окрик Станиславского: «Свет!» Зал вздрогнул, шум, переполох. Судейкин и Сапунов вскакивают с мест, возражают. Голос Станиславского: «Публика не может долго выносить мрак на сцене, это не психологично, нужно видеть лица актеров!»…Судейкин и Сапунов: «Но декорация рассчитана на полумрак, на свету она теряет весь художественный смысл!»…Наступает опять тишина, в которой бьется размеренная речь актеров, но уже при полном освещении сцены. Но едва дали свет, как погибла вся декорация, началось расхождение, разнобой живописи и фигур действующих лиц. Станиславский встает, за ним встают зрители. Репетиция оборвана, постановка не принята (201).

[16] На сцене семь принцесс сидят в семи беседках трельяжа, сквозь которые сверкает небо в облаках барашках. За сценой музыка Глиера. Семь принцесс вышивают единую золотую ленту во всю длину сцены, композиционно объединяющую их. Громкие аплодисменты сначала первых рядов, затем всего зрительного зала. Я вздрогнул. Аплодисменты мне, художнику, показавшему первый раз свой силы в декоративной области. Это ободрило меня и мне показалось, что тревога всей труппы за будущность театра совершенно напрасна, все обойдется как надо…(202).

[17]Вожможно ли открывать театр с репертуаром, не отве-
чающим настроению масс? (200).

[18]Для меня было личной драмой то, что Станиславский за-
крыл в 1905 году студию на Поварской, но в сущности он
был прав. По свойственным мне торопливости и безогляд-
ности я стремился там соединить в одно самые разнородные
элементы: символистскую драматургию, художников- стили-
заторов и актерскую молодежь, воспитанную по школе ран-
него Художественного театра. Каковы бы ни были задачи,
это все вместе не соединялось и, грубо говоря, напоминало
басню «Лебедь, рак и щука». Станиславский, с его чутьем и
вкусом, понял это, а для меня, когда я опомнился от горечи
неудачи, это стало уроком: сначала надо воспитать нового
актера, а уж потом ставить перед ним новые задачи. Такой
же вывод сделал и Станиславский, в сознании котор-ого
тогда уже зрели черты его «системы» в ее первой ре-дакции
(*Станиславский* 71–72).

Chapter Two

[1]Benedetti attributes this information to a series of manuscripts which
were finally published in 1922 under the title *Various Trends in
Dramatic Art* (191).

[2]Душой студии являлся Л. А. Сулержицкий. Круг обязан-
ностей этого человека определить было очень трудно. Это
был и директор студии, и «классный наставник», и админи-
стратор, и электромонтёр (если портрился свет,) и автор бес-
конечного ряда сценариев для упражнений, импровизаций, и
художник-плакатист, если нужно было вывесить в студии
какой-нибудь плакат (91).

[3]The Dukhobors were a Russian religious sect which separated from the
Orthodox Church in 1785. Many Dukhobors emigrated to Canada in the
1890's to escape persecution.

[4]For a more detailed account of the process by which Vakhtangov
entered the Moscow Art Theatre, see Chapter 4.

[5]Почему он так полюбил Студию? Потому что она осуществляла одну из главных его жизненных целей: сближать людей между собой, создавать общее дело, общие цели, общий труд и радость, бороться с пошлостью, насилием и несправедливостью, служить любви и природе, красоте и богу (Станиславский на Маркова 256).

[6]Это не могло не передаваться зрителям, когда они смотрели, как играют актеры, сгруппировавшиеся вокруг этого странного и вдохновенного человека. Потому и нужна была форма студии—форма содружества и тесного, замкнутого сближения,—чтобы полнее и сосредоточеннее передать зрителю то, что Сулержицкий нес с собой и что он будил в ощущениях тех, с кем работал. Он стремился в театре к самому верному и самому правдивому и потому, казалось, часто грешил против театральности (255).

[7]Студия формулировала свои задачи так: 1) развитие психологии актерского творчества, 2) выработка актерского самочуствия и 3) сближение актера с автором. Правда актерского исполнения была подчеркнута внешне вынуденым, а внутренне органичным в то время устройством сцены без рампы и подмосков (Марков 270).

[8]В «Сверчке на печи», нет простых и цельных натур, нет идеализации прошлого, примирения человека с действительностью. В его постановках раскрывалась жизнь страдающего и обреченного человека, исковерканного капиталистическим городомж не идеализация прошлого, а беспощадный показ современности интересует Вахтангова (17).

[9]For a more complete discussion of this conflict between Stanislavsky and Nemirovich-Danchenko, see the Introduction.

[10]Skobelevsky Square was later known as Soviet Square.

[11]Так родилась знаменитая песенка в «Потопе» и найден был наконец, ключ к сцене единения. Не через мысли о любви и добре, не через слова о покаянии и примирении, а через подсознательное, полуживотное, получеловеческое мы-чание людей, сбившихся в кучу от ужаса смерти. Быстрее, громче!...Тепер уже радостнее. Почуствовав себя вместе, они уже не так испуганы. Им передается тепло и ритм друг

друга, захватывает физиологическое ощущение жизни и
взаимной поддержки (121)

[12]The reorganization of the Moscow Art Theatre and its Studios is
discussed in more detail in Chapter Three.

Chapter Three

[1]On page 221 of his biography of Stanislavsky, Jean Benedetti refers to
this production as *The Golden Ring*. I believe this must be a mistaken
translation of the word *зелёное*, meaning green, which is very similar to
золотое, meaning gold or golden.

[2]Актеры—юноши, девушки семнадцати-девятнадцати лет,
впервые встретившиеся с руководителем Художественного
театра...Вот. Он, Станиславский, в этом маленьком поме-
щении, окруженный молодыми, смущенными лицами. Толпа
полудетей ждет от него решения их судьбы (103).

[3]The Julian (Old Style) Calendar was used in Russia until 1918, at
which time Russia converted to the Gregorian (New Style) calendar
which was 13 days ahead at the time of the change. Therefore, the
February Revolution occurred in March, New Style and the October
Revolution was in November, New Style.

[4]Играли в холодных, нетепленых помещениях. Зрители, си-
девшие в пальто, в валенках, принимали самое активнное
участие в ходе спектакля, нередко громко реагируя на то
или иное событие. Но нас это не смущало, так как мы чуст-
вовали громадную непосредственную заинтересованность
зрительного зала во всем происходящем на сцене, видели
сотни горящих любознательных глаз, устремеленых на нас
(Виноградская 386).

[5]Нам предоставляли самим прокладывать свой путь. В
студии действовал закон, справедлвость которого я поняла
много позже: научить нельзя, научиться можно. И еще один
закон: проявляйте инициативу. Никто за тебя ничего не
сделает, если ты сам не вложишь в работу полную меру
своей души, таланта, изобретательности, не будешь сам

искать для себя отрывки, не будешь готовить их, показываться и т.д. Но если ты будешь инициативен и настойчив, то всегда получишь нужный совет и помощь (144).

[6]Актриса не очень большого дарования, она была исключительно тонким и талантливым воспитателем молодых актеров. Она умела быть настоящим другом актера, чутким, но не чувствительным, внимательным, но не сентиментальным, умеющим видеть в утенке будущего лебедя и помогать его рождению. Как никто, умела она помочь сложному процессу кристализации, происходящему в душе будущего актера, вложить в него высокие этические и эстетические нормы. Тогда, когда душа жаждет, чтобы в нее что-то вкладывали. Она умела делать это с великим тактом (145).

[7]This long and complicated title is directly translated as: *The story about Ivan the fool and his two brothers: Simeon the Warrior and Fat Taras, and their Deaf Sister Malane, and about the old devil and three imps.* In the Russian, this title is abbreviated as *"Сказка"* or *"Story."* For the purposes of this book, it will be abbreviated as *"Ivan the Fool."*

[8]Слишком затянулся период работы над спектаклье—менялись режиссеры, и поэтому, блестяще решенный в отдельных частях, спектакль не был единым по замыслу. Кроме того, за четыре года жизни студия уже сформировала свой зрительный зал, желавший продолжения линии «Зелен-ого кольца» и «Младости». Переход от спектаклей интимно-камерных, психологических к зрелищу условному, грубому для многих оказался неожиданным и нежел-ательным. Тем не менее именно «Сказка» стала переломным моментом в переходе студии от детства к зрелости. Общение в непосредственной и длительной работе с такими мастерами режиссуры, как Вахтангов и Станиславский, с таким педагогом, как М. А. Чехов, поиски формы спектакля, выход в мир народной раскрепощенной фантазии—все это не проходит бесследно и заставляет, вольно или невольно, взрослеть (107).

[9]See Chapter Four

[10]Предоставленная сама себе, Вторая студия увлекалась экспериментами и поисками... (107).

[11]Казалось, вместе с лицом Хмелев сделал себе новую душу, новый ход мыслей (165).

[12]Было непостижимо, как совсемюный актер, почти маль-чик, выросшии в рабочем пригороде, застенчивый и не-людимый, делал абсолютно своим, пережитым до мель-чайших деталей сложнейший внутренний мир Шпигельберга. Как достигал он такой всепоглощающей веры в собственную избранность, исключительность, в то, что именно ему высшей силой предначертано вести за собой толпу в неведомое царство (165)?

[13]Вторая студия сдала «Разбойников». Самостоятельно.... Я не скрыл, что мне спектакль не нравится решительно.... Спектакль какой-то неприятный. Нарочитая левизна, внешняя, вздорная, дешевая: то есть конструктивизм, чудища вместо людей и пр.... Актеры по-актерски недурны...А внешность не-приятная (167).

Chapter Four

[1]Между этим двумя датами лежит жизнь яркая, талант-ливая, полная творческого огня и подлинного вдохновения (Куза 5).

[2]At one time also known as Ordjonikidze

[3]ярко освещенном мире, где соединяются жизнь и фантазия и где артист сливается в творческом порыве с целым кол-лективом на сцене и со зрителями в зале (Херсонский 35).

[4]It is interesting to note that at this time in his career Vakhtangov's wife Nadezhda took a very active role in support of her husband. For this amateur production she played Rima, the sister of Vakhtangov's character, Georgii.

[5]Хочу образовать студию, где бы мы учились. Принцип— всего добиваться самим. Руководитель—все. Проверить сис-тему К. С. на самих себе. Принять или отвергнуть ее. Ис-править, дополнить или убрать ложь. Все, пришедшие в

студию, должны любить искусство вообще и сценическое в частности. Радость искать в творчестве. Забыть публику. Творить для себя. Наслаждаться для себя. Сами себе судьи (77).

[6]A second-rate imitator or follower, especially of an artist or philosopher (*The American Heritage Dictionary, 3rd Edition*).

[7]Вахтангов был подлинным сыном Художественного театра, но сыном непокорным. Дух эпигонства, дух безыдейного и ремесленого подражания великим мастерам был чужд Вахтангову (6)

[8]Станиславский совсем не владеет театральной формой в благородном значении этого слова. Он мастер на образы и неожиданные приспособления действующих лиц, но совсем не мастер форм театрального представления. Поэтому он и омещанил театр, убрав кричащий занавес, убрав выходы ак-теров, убрав оркестр, убрав всякую театральность (Рудницкий «Всехсвятские записи» 150).

[9]In the text of his book, Simonov dates the original production of *St. Anthony* as 1916 (129) but his chronology agrees with that in Khersonsky, dating the premiere of *St. Anthony* as September 15, 1918. The confusion could lie in the fact that in Russian theatres the rehearsal period for a play is often quite long and it is possible that Vakhtangov did indeed "choose *The Miracle of St. Anthony* in 1916 for his work in his own studio" (Simonov 129) but that the play was not performed for the public until September of 1918.

[10]Актерам надо не только психологически правдиво показать этих Ашиллей и Гюставов: надо и ясно определить их об-щие основные классовые черты. (226).

[11]Королевская власть рано или позно гибнет в силу своих внутренних противоречий... конфликтом между желанием стать демократическим добрым «отцом народа» и необ-ходимостью опираться на феодальную знать и подчинять свои действия ее интересам... Эрик не может до конца разрешить своих конфликтов ни со знатью, ни с народом (крестьянами,) ни с близкими людьми. Гибель такого Эрика—человека на троне была неизбежной. Трон стал для Эрика эшафотом. Гибель такого короля, дерзнувшего быть человеком, была показана не в реальных, убедительных конкретно-

исторических условиях, а в отвлеченной, экспрессионистской трактовке (Херсонский 228—233).

[12]Линия надреза идет между двух миров—не между небом (мистическими представлениями или пусть хотя бы поэтической абстракцией) и землей и не просто между миром бедняков и богачей, но между живыми, реальными человеческими чуствами и судьбами, с одной стороны, и проклятым миром прошлого с его бытом, религией, законами— с другой. Человек не может жить, не может сохранить свою прекрасную живую душу в мире угнетения, уродства и страха (246).

[13]не разрабатывает значительной социальной темы, а сосредоточивает свое внимание на нахождении принципов нового театра и его выразительных средств, на поисках формы романтического представления (Зорграф 124).

[14]Vakhtangov's death was caused by a combination of tuberculosis and stomach cancer with which he had struggled for many years.

[15]Симонов, *Вахтангов: 20 лет*, глава "Путь Театра".

APPENDIX

Repertoire of the First Studio

Wreck of the Ship "Hope," Drama in four acts by H. Heijermans.
Translation: A. P. Vorotnikov and E. E. Matterna.
Director: R. V. Boleslavsky.
Designer: Ia. I. Gremislavskii.
In the programs for 1916 P. G. Uzunov.
In the programs for the 1920's: "Scenic designers M. V. Libakov and P. G. Uzunov."
Premiere: January 15/28 1913.
Total number of performances: 429 + 25 = 454.

Holiday of Peace, Play in three acts by G. Hauptman. Translation: L. M. Vasilevskii.
Director: E. B. Vakhtangov.
Scene design: M. V. Libakov.
Music: N. N. Rakhmanov.
Premiere: October 15/28, 1913.
Total number of performances: 96.

Cricket on the Hearth, Christmas Story (four scenes) by C. Dickens.
Adapted for the stage by B. M. Sushkevich.
Director: B. M. Sushkevich.
Scene designers: M. B. Libakov and P. G. Uzunov.
In the programs of the 1920's: "scenery by M. V. Libakov"
Music: N. N. Rakhmanov.
Premiere: November 24/December 7 1914.
Total number of performances: 509 + 33 = 542.

Travels of the Invalids, Tragedy in three acts by V. M. Volkenshtein.
Director: R. V. Boleslavsky.
Designers: M. V. Libakov and P. G. Uzunov.
Music from old songs: N. N. Rakhmanov.

Premiere: December 22 1914/ January 4 1915.
Total number of performances: 55.

Flood, Play in three acts by G. Berger.
Translation: V. L. Binshtok and Z. A. Vengerov.
Director: E. B. Vakhtangov.
Designers: M. V. Libakov and P. G. Uzunov.
Premiere: December 14/27, 1915.
Total number of performances: $396 + 31 = 427$.

An Evening of Anton Pavlovich Chekhov: *The Proposal*, a joke in one act; *On the Dangers of Tobacco*, a monologue; *The Witch*, a staged story; *Anniversary*, a joke in one act.
Directors: V. L. Mchedelov, V. V. Gotovtsev.
Designers: A. V. Andreev (*The Proposal* and *The Witch*) and P. G. Uzunov (*Anniversary*).
Wigs: Ia. I. Gremlislavskii.
Premiere: March 22/April 4 1916.
Total number of performances: 147.

Swan Song (*Kalkhas*), Dramatic etude by A. P. Chekhov. (Together with *The Proposal*, *The Witch* and *Anniversary*). Directors/Performers: L. M. Leonidov and N. F. Kolin.
Premiere: April 19/May 2 1917

Incurable, excerpt by G. I. Uspenskii (together with the pieces by A. P. Chekhov *On the Dangers of Tobacco, The Witch, Anniversary).*
Directors/Performers: A. I. Cheban and A. D. Popov
Premiere: May 16/29 1916.

Twelfth Night, or What you Will, Comedy in three acts (thirteen scenes)by W. Shakespeare.
Translation: P. E. Wineberg.
Production supervisor: K. S. Stanislavsky
Director: B. M. Sushkevich.
Scenic designer: A. V. Andreev.
In programs from the 1920's: "Scenic designer M. V. Libakov"
Wigs: Ia. I. Gremislavskii.
Music: N. N. Rakhmanov.
Premiere: November 21/ December 4 1917.
Total number of performances: 221

Rosmersholm, Play in three acts by H. Ibsen.
Translation: A. V. and P. G. Ganzen.

Director: E. B. Vakhtangov.
Scenic Designer: M. V. Libakov.
Premiere: May 14, 1918.
Total number of performances: 19.

The Daughter of Jorio Pastoral tragedy in three acts by
G. D'Annunzio,
Translation: A. P. Vorotnikov.
Directors: N. N. Bromlei and L. I. Deikun.
Scenic design: P. G. Uzunov.
Music: N. N. Rakhmanov.
Premiere: January 20, 1919.
Total number of performances: 80.

Balladina, Dramatic poem in four acts (eleven scenes) by
Iu. Slovatskii.
Translation: K. D. Balmont.
Staging: R. V. Boleslavsky.
Designer: R. V. Boleslavsky.
Composor: N. N. Rakhmanov.
Premiere: February 16, 1920.
Total number of performances: $72 + 27 = 99$.

Erik XIV, Play in four acts by A. Strindberg.
Translation: Iu. A. Veselovskii.
Staging: E. B. Vakhtangov.
Directors: E. B. Vakhtangov and B. M. Sushkevich.
Designer: I. I. Nivinskii.
Music: N. N. Rakhmanov.
Premiere: March 29, 1921
Total number of performances: $76 + 31 = 107$.

The Archangel Michael, Tragic farce in four acts by N. N. Bromlei.
Staging: B. M. Sushkevich.
Directors: N. N. Bromlei and B. M. Sushkevich.
Designer: V. M. Khodasevich.
Scenery implementation: M. V. Libakov and A. I. Blagonravov.
Music: N. N. Rakhmanov.
Premiere: June 3, 1922.
The play was given five general rehearsals.
This play was not included in the repertoire.

Hero, Comedy in three acts by J. M. Synge.
Translation: K. I. Chukovskii.

Director: A. D. Dikii.
Designer: A. A. Radakov and M. V. Libakov.
Costumes created from sketches by A. A. Radakov under the supervision of M. F. Mikhailova.
Headdresses: I. S. Alekseeva.
Wigs: N. A. Alekseev.
Music: N. N. Rakhmanov
Premiere: January 17, 1923.
Total number of performances: 23.

Taming of the Shrew, Comedy in three acts with a prologue and epilogue by W. Shakespeare.
Translation: P. P. Gnedich.
Staging: V. S. Smyshlyaev.
Directors: A. I. Cheban and V. S. Smyshlyaev.
Designer: B. A. Matrunin.
Costumes from sketches by Matrunin created by A. G. Silich, K. N. Ushakov and M. F. Mikhailova.
Headdresses: I. S. Alekseeva and N. S. Smirnova.
Wigs and Hair: N. A. Alekseev.
Music: S. A. Kondrateva.
Conductor: N. N. Rakhmanov
Premiere: April 4, 1923.
Total number of performances: 52.

King Lear, Tragedy in five acts (thirteen scenes) by W. Shakespeare.
Translation: A. V. Druzhinin.
Director: B. M. Sushkevich.
Designer: K. N. Istomin.
Composor: V. A. Oranskii.
Conductor: N. N. Rakhmanov.
Costumes: M. G. Avdveeva and M. F. Mikhailova.
Headdresses: I. S. Alekseeva.
Wigs and Hair: N. A. Alekseev.
Machines for sound effects invented by V. A. Popov.
Premiere: May 23, 1923.
Total number of performances: 29.

Love—The Golden Book, Play in three acts by A. N. Tolstoy.
Director: S. G. Birman.
Designer: D. N. Kardovsky.
Costumes: M. F. Mikhailova.
Wigs and Hair: N. A. Alekseev.

Premiere: January 3, 1924.
Total number of performances: 30.

The Wastrel, Drama (five scenes)by N. S. Leskov.
Staging: B. M. Sushkevich.
Directors: N. N. Bromlei and A. D. Dikii.
Designer: A. A. Geirot.
Chorus: K. S. Stanislavsky Opera Studio under the direction of S. A. Krynkin.
Choirmaster: A. S. Stepanov.
Costumes: M. F. Mikhailova and K. N. Ushakov.
Premiere: March 15, 1924.
Total number of performances: 10.

Also preserved in the archives of the Moscow Art Theatre Museum is the following poster:

"Production by the artists of the First studio of Moscow Art and Academic Theatre" in the facilities of the Bat theatre:
The End of the Story, and *The Great Question*, J. London, *The Potentate's Fate*, B. Show
Premiere: December 3, 1918
Played again on December 7, 1918 (as given on the poster).

Repertoire of the Second Studio

The Green Ring, Play in four acts by Z. N. Gippius.
Director: V. L. Mchedelov.
Designers: S. B. Nikritin, A. V. Sokolov.
Final rehearsals taken by K. S. Stanislavsky.
Premiere: November 24, 1916.
Continued in Moscow until June 2, 1922.
Total number of performances: 401

Studio Diary, staged excerpts from the novels by N. S. Leskov; *No Way Out* and *The Story of Lieutenant Ergunov* with three scenes from I. S. Turgenev and compositions from *White Nights* by F. M. Dostoevsky.
Director/teachers and adaptors: E. F. Krasnopolskaya and N. O. Massalitinov.
Premiere: February 14, 1918.

Studio Diary, staged excerpts from *Thieves* by A. Chekhov and *A Comedy about a Man who Married a Dumb Wife* by A. France

Translation: N. P. Aslanov
Director/teacher: V. L. Mchedelov
Designer: M. P. Gortinskaya
Premiere: March 1919

Later versions of *Studio Diary* included staged excerpts from the stories *Ivan Matveevich, Egor, The Criminal,* and *Long Tongue* by A. Chekhov and *The Story of Two Ladies* from *Dead Souls* by N. V. Gogol
Director: E. B. Vakhtangov

During the 1918/19 season, the studio members gave fifteen concert performances accompanied by lectures by Professor P. N. Sakulin. Pieces by N. V. Gogol, N. A. Nekrasov, I. S. Nikitina, A. V. Koltsov, A. P. Chekhov and others were prepared and performed under the direction of the Studio pedagogues.

Youth, Play in five scenes by L. Andreev.
Directors: N. N. Litovtseva and V. L. Mchedelov.
Finish work on the piece by K. S. Stanislavsky.
Designer: V. N. Masiutin.
Scenery constructed by S. N. Nikolskii
Music: S. I. Pototskii.
Premiere: December 13, 1918.
Final performance in Moscow: April 22, 1924.
Total number of performances: 371.

The Rose Pattern, drama in 5 acts (six scenes) by F. Sologub, adapted by the author for the theatre from the novel *Miss Liza.*
Director: V. V. Luzhskii.
Designer: M. P. Gortinskaya.
Scenery constructed by: B. A. Matrunin
Music: S. I. Pototskii.
Premiere: March 19, 1920.
Last performance in Moscow: March 23, 1924
Total number of performances: 219.

The Story of Ivan the Fool and his Brothers, Play in eight scenes taken from the story by L. N. Tolstoy.
Adapted for the stage by: M. A. Chekhov
Staging: K. S. Stanislavsky.
Director: B. I. Vershilov.
Designer: B. A. Matrunin.
Costumes: K. N. Ushakov
Wigs: M. G. Faleev

Composer: Iu. S. Sakhovskii.
Premiere: March 22, 1922.
After the Studio closed, the production moved to the Small stage of the Moscow Art and Academic Theatre.
Final performance in Moscow: September 17, 1928.
Total number of performances in Moscow: 138.

The Robbers by F. Schiller.
Translated and transformed into verse with an additional epilogue by P. G. Antokol'skii.
Staging: B. I. Vershilov.
Directors: B. I. Vershilov, E. S. Telesheva and E. K. Elina.
Designer: V. L. Iustitskii.
Costumes: K. N. Ushakov and T. I. Osipova
Wigs: M. I. Chernova
Composer: V. A. Oranskii.
Premiere: March 6, 1923.
Final performance in Moscow: May 11, 1923
Total number of performances: 42.

Storm by A. N. Ostrovsky.
Staging: I. Ia Sudakov.
Director: E. S. Telesheva.
Designer: B. A. Matrunin.
Composer: V. A. Oranskii.
Premiere: April 13, 1923.
Final performance in Moscow: May 10, 1924.
Total number of performances in Moscow: 45.

The Invisible Woman, Comedy in three acts by P. Calderone.
Translation: K. Bal'mont.
Staging: B. I. Vershilov.
Director: L. I. Zueva.
Designer: I. I. Nivinskii.
Costumes: N. P. Lamanova
Choreographer: L. A. Lashchilin
Stage Combat: E. E. Pons
Composer: V. A. Oranskii.
Premiere: April 9, 1924.
Following the end of the Studio's independent work, the production moved to the Small stage of the Moscow Art and Academic Theatre.
Final performance: March 16, 1927.
Total number of performances: 154.

Elizabeth Petrovna, Tragi-comedy of palace intrigues in five acts by D. P. Smolin. Produced in memory of V. L. Mchedelov
Staging: L. V. Baratov
Directors: L. V. Baratov, V. L. Mchedelov, E. S. Telesheva, V. Ia. Stanitsin.
Designer: S. I. Ivanov.
Wigs: M. G. Faleev and M. I. Chernova
Music after authentic material reworked by Iu. S. Sakhnovskii.
Premiere: March 29, 1925 on the Small stage of the Moscow Art and Academic Theatre.
Final performance: May 24, 1934.
Total number of performances: 310.

Studio tours:
1919, Simbirsk
1920, Ekaterinoslav
1921, Briansk
1922, Tiflis
1923, Baku, Tiflis, Petrograd
1924, Nizhni Novgorod, Kazan, Samar, Saratov
1926, Sverdlovsk, Novo-Nikolaevska

Tour repertoire was made up of specially prepared plays or scenes. For example, in the summer of 1919, E. B. Vakhtangov directed the Second Studio in *Flood* by Berger. Also intended for the tour was such student work as the vaudeville *Nedomorok (Small Size)* (*Недоморок*)by D. Nikkodemi, the adaptation for the stage of *Ryleev's Interrogation* (*Допрос Рылеева*) from the novel *December 14* (*14 Декабря*) by D. S. Merezhkovskii, and others.

The independent existence of the Second Studio is considered to have ended on September 1, 1924.

Those from the Second Studio who joined with the Moscow Art and Academic Theatre were: A. M. Azarin, E. A. Aleeva, O. N. Androvskaya, N. P. Batalov, V. A. Verbitskii, B. I. Vershilov, S. N. Garrel', G. A. Gerasimov, A. I. Guzeev, N. S. Devichenskii, K. N. Elanskei, A. P. Zueva, L. I. Zueva, E. M. Zelenova, V. P. Istrin, E. V. Kaluzhskii, M. N. Kedrov, M. O. Knebel', a. M. Komissarov, O. N. Labzina, P. V. Lecli, N. V. Mikhalovskaia, B. A. Mordvinov, A. B. Petrova, M. I. Prudkin, M. I. Puzyreva, I. M. Raevskii, V. S. Sokolova, V. Ia. Stanitsin, I. Ia. Sudakov, A. K. Tarasova, E. S. Telesheva, M. A. Titova, N. P. Khmelev, M. A. Tsenovskaia, O. Ia. Iakubovskaia, M. M. Ianshin.

Repertoire of the Third Studio

The Miracle of St. Anthony, Comedy by M. Maeterlinck.
Translation: A. Vorotnikov.
Staging: E. B. Vakhtangov.
Designer: Iu. A. Zavadskii.
Premiere: November 13, 1921
Total number of performances: 149.

An Evening of A. P. Chekhov (Thieves, Anniversary, Wedding)
Staging: E. B. Vakhtangov.
Premiere: November 15, 1921.
Total number of performances: 32.

Princess Turandot, from the story by Carlo Gozzi.
Translation: M. A. Osorgin.
Staging: E. B. Vakhtangov.
Directors: K. I. Kotlubai, Iu. A. Zavadskii, B. E. Zakhava.
Designer: I. I. Invinskii.
Music: N. I. Sizov, A. D. Kozlovskii.
Premiere: February 27, 1922.
This production moved to the Vakhtangov Theatre in 1997

Truth is Good, but Happiness is Better, Comedy by A. N. Ostrovsky.
Director: B. E. Zakhava.
Designer: S. P. Isakov.
Premiere: March 20, 1923.
Total number of performances: 68.

The Wedding, Comedy by N. V. Gogol.
Staging: Iu. A. Zavadskii.
Director: B. V. Shchukin.
Designer: S. P. Isakov.
Music: N. I. Sizov.
Premiere: January 29, 1924.
Total number of performances: 39.

Comedy Merime, from the cycle *The Theatre of Klara Gazul'*.
1. *Heaven and Hell*, 2. *African Love*, 3. *The Cart of Holy Gifts*
4. *She-devil*.
Translation: V. Khodasevich.
Staging: A. D. Popov.
Directors: L. G. Antokol'skii, N. M. Gorchakov.
Designer: I. I. Nivinskii.

Music: N. S. Sizov.
Premiere: September 19, 1924.
Total number of performances: 124.

Lev Gurych Sinichkin, Old vaudeville by D. T. Lenskii.
Text alterations: N. R. Erdman.
Staging: R. N. Simonov.
Director: O. N. Basov.
Designer: B. F. Erdman.
Music: A. N. Verstovskii.
Adaptation and insertions: N. I. Sizov.
Premiere: December 16, 1924.
Total number of performances: 279.

Virineia, Scenes from country life by L. N. Seifullina and V. L. Pravdukhin.
Staging: A. D. Popov.
Director: I. M. Tolchanov.
Designer: S. P. Isakov
Premiere: October 13, 1925.
Total number of performances: 143.

Marion de Lorm, Melodrama by V. Hugo.
Translation: N. L. Rossov.
Staging: R. N. Simonov.
Directors: P. G. Antokol'skii, B. V. Shchukin.
Designer: I. I. Nivinskii.
Music: N. I. Sizov.
Premiere: January 26, 1926
Total number of performances: 69

Zoika's Apartment, Play by M. A. Bulgakov.
Director: A. D. Popov.
Designer: S. P. Isakov.
Musical and Sound montage: A. D. Kozlovskii.
Premiere: October 28, 1926.
Total number of performances: 200.

BIBLIOGRAPHY

Works Cited

English

Benedetti, Jean, trs. and ed. *The Moscow Art Theatre Letters*. New York: Routledge, 1991.

_____. *Stanislavski*. New York: Routledge, 1988.

Gordon, Mel. *The Stanislavsky Technique: Russia*. New York: Applause, 1987.

Hoover, Marjorie L. *Meyerhold The Art of Conscious Theatre*. Amherst: U of Massachusetts, 1974.

Orani, Aviv. "Realism in Vakhtangov's Theatre of Fantasy" *Theatre Journal*. December 1984.

Polyakova, Elena. *Stanislavsky*. Moscow: Progress, 1982.

Rudnitsky, Konstantin. *Meyerhold the Director*. George Petrov trs. Sydney Schultze ed. Ann Arbor: Ardis, 1981.

_____. *Russian and Soviet Theater 1905-1932*. Roxane Permar trs. Dr. Lesley Milne ed. New York: Harry N. Abrams, 1988.

Shaw, J. Thomas. *The Transliteration of Modern Russian for English-Language Publications*. Madison: U of Wisconsin P, 1967.

Simonov, Ruben. *Stanislavsky's Protégé: Eugene Vakhtangov*. Miriam Goldina trs. Helen Choat ed. New York: Drama Book Specialists, 1969.

Smeliansky, Anatoly M. *Is Comrade Bulgakov Dead? Mikhail Bulgakov at the Moscow Art Theatre.* Arch Tait trs. New York: Routledge, 1993.

Stanislavski, Constantin. *My Life in Art.* J. J. Robbins trs. New York: Theatre Arts Books, 1948.

Russian

Варпаховский, Л. *Музыка в драматическом театре.* Л: Мукзыка Ленинград, 1976.

Веригина, В. П. «Воспоминания» В сб. *О Станиславском.* М: ВТО, 1948.

_____. *Встречи с Мейерхольдом.* М: ВТО, 1967.

Виноградская, И. Н. «Вторая Студия Московского Художественного Театра» в сб. *Советский Театр Документы и Материалы 1917–1967.* Л: 1968.

Зорграф, Н. *Вахтангов.* М: Искусство, 1939.

Иванова, М. «Уроки Второй Студии» *Театр.* 1 (1972): 99–110.

Кнебель, М. *Все Жизнь.* М: ВТО, 1967.

Куза, В. В. *Государственный Театр имени Евг. Вахтангова.* М: Издание Музея Театра, 1940.

Марков, П. *Правда Театра.* М: Искусство, 1965

Мелик-Захаров, С. В. и Ш. Ш. Богатырев ред. *Станиславский.* М: Искусство, 1963.

Попов, А. Д. «Воспоминания и размышления» *Театр.* 2 (1960)

Попов, С. А. «Воспоминания» В сб. *О Станиславском.* М: ВТО, 1948.

Пыжова, О. И. *Призвание*. М: Искусство, 1974.

Рудницкий, К. «Всехсвятские Записи» *Театр*. (1987): 147–151.

Симонов, Р. *Театр Имени Евг. Вахтангова 20 лет*. М: Музея театра, 1946.

Станиславский, К. С. *Стати, Речи, Беседы Писма*. М: Искусство, 1953.

Улянов, Н. П. *Мой встречи, воспоминания*. М: Академии Художесть СССР, 1952.

Херсонский, Х. *Вахтангов*. Москва: Молодая Гвардия, 1940.

Works Consulted

English

Black, Lendley C. *Mikhail Chekhov as Actor, Director, and Teacher*. Ann Arbor, UMI, 1987.

Boleslavsky, Richard. *Acting: The First Six Lessons*. New York: Theatre Arts Books, 1933.

Brockett, Oscar G. and Robert Findlay. *Century of Innovation Second Edition*. Boston: Allyn and Bacon, 1991.

Chekhov, Michael. *On the Technique of Acting*. Mel Gordon ed. New York: Harper, 1991.

Hingley, Ronald. *Russia A Concise History*. London: Thames and Hudson, 1991.

Mirsky, D. S. *A History of Russian Literature from its Beginnings to 1900*. Francis J. Whitfield ed. New York: Vintage Books, 1958.

Morgan, Joyce Vining. *Stanislavski's Encounter with Shakespeare: The Evolution of a Method*. Diss. Yale U, 1980. Ann Arbor: UMI, 1980. 8025218

Munk, Erika ed. *Stanislavski and America*. New York: Hill and Wang, 1966

Nemirovitch-Dantchenko, Vladimir. *My Life in the Russian Theatre*. John Cournos trs. New York: Theatre Arts, 1936.

Slonim, Marc. *Russian Theatre From the Empire to the Soviets*. Cleveland: World, 1961.

Stanislavski, Konstantin Sergeevich. *An Actor's Handbook: An Alphabetical Arrangement of Concise Statements on Aspects of Acting*. Elizabeth Reynolds Hapgood trs. New York: Theatre Arts, 1963.

_____. *Stanislavsky on the Art of the Stage*. David Magarshack trs. New York: Hill and Wang, 1961

_____. *Selected Works*: Oksana Korneva ed. Vladimir Yankilevsky trs. Moscow: Raduga, 1984

_____. *Building a Character*. Elizabeth Reynolds Hapgood trs. New York: Theatre Arts, 1949.

Velekova, Nina. *Moscow Theatres A Pictorial Guide*. Melinda Maclain trs. Moscow: Planeta, 1979.

Russian

Балатова, Н. «Искания Первой Студии.» *Театр* 3 (1975): 122–127.

Бассехес, А. *Художники на Сцене МХАТ*. М: ВТО, 1960.

Бирман, С. *Пут Актрисы*. М: ВТО, 1959.

Брюсов, В. «*Смерть Тентажиля* по Метерлинку.» *Весы* 12 (1905).

Вахтангов Материалы и Статьи. М: ВТО, 1959.

Виноградская, П. «Октябрь в Москве.» *Новый Мир* 4 (1966): 143–186.

Волков, Н. *Мейерхольд.* М: Академиа, 1929.

Волин, В. «*Гибель Надежды.*» *Культура Театра* 5 (1921): 54–55.

_____. «Три Студии.» *Театральное Обозрение* 7 (1921): 4–5.

«Вторая Студия МХТ» *Театр и Студия* 1–2 (1922): 71.

«Вторая Студия МХТ» *Театр и Музыка* 17 (1922): 25.

Гиацинтова, С. *Памятью Наедине.* М: Искусство, 1989.

Глумов, А. *Нестертые Строхи.* М: ВТО, 1977.

Гочаков, Н. *Режиссорские Уроки Вахтангова.* М: Искусство, 1957.

_____. *Режиссёрские Уроки К. С. Станиславского Беседы и Записи репетиций.* М: Искусство, 1951.

Громов, В. *Михаил Чехов.* М: Искусство, 1970.

Давыдова, М. *Советские Художники театра и кино.* 1977.

Данилевич, Л. «Искусство Жизненной правды.» *О Русской Советской Музыке.* М: Советский Композитор, 1975.

Дикий, А. *Избранное.* М: ВТО, 1976.

_____. *Повесть О Театральной Юности.* М: Искусство. 1957.

Дрейден, С. «В. И. Ленин Смотрит Потоп.» *Нева* 7 (1967): 197–205.

_____. *В Зрительном Зале.* М: Искусство, 1967.

Жаров, М. *Жизнь, Театр, Кино Воспоминания*. М: Искусство, 1967.

Завадский, Ю. *Учителя и Ученики*. М: Искусство, 1975.

Захава, Б. *Современики*. М: Искусство, 1969.

_____. *Вахтангов и его студия*. Л: 1930.

История Советского драматического Театра Том I 1917–1920. М: Наука, 1966.

Зиновьев, Н. *Жизнь Искусства* 28 (1925): 21.

Зорграф, М. *Малй Театр в Конце XIX-Начале XX века*. М: Наука, 1966.

_____. и Ю. С. Калашников, П.А. Марков, Б. И. Ростоцкий ред. *Очерки Истории Русского Советского Драматического Театра Том I 1917–1934*. М: ИАН СССР, 1954.

Иванова, М. *Вторая Студия и Процесс Обновления Риализма МХАТ*. М: ВНИИ, 1978.

Израилевский, Б. *Музыка в Спектаклях Московского Художественного Театра*. М: ВТО, 1965.

Капитайкин, Э. «О Студийности.» *Режиссура в Пути*. Л: Искусство, 1966.

Коган, Д. *Сергей Юрывич Судейкин 1884–1946*. М: Искусство, 1974.

Комиссаржевский, В. «Театр как Коллектив» *Вопросы режиссуры*. М: Искусство, 1954.

Куров, Н. «*Гибель Надежды.*» *Театр* 1230 (1913): 6.

Леонидов, О. «В Мансуровской.» *Театральный Курыр* 20 (1918) 5–6.

Марков, П. «II Студия Сказка об Иване—Дураке.» *Театральное Обозрение* 5 (1922): 6.

Михаильский, Ф. «На спектакле *Свечок на Печи.*» *Документы и Воспоминания.* Л: Искусство, 1970.

«Московский Художествений Театр.» *Жизнь Искусство* 110 (1919): 3.

Нежанов, Л. «Двор во II Худож. Театре» *Рабис* 21 (1930): 9.

Нежный, И. *Былое Перед Глазами.* М: ВТО, 1963.

Немирович-Данченко, В. И. *К. С. Станиславскому Осень 1905 Избранные Писма.* М: Искусство, 1954.

_____. *Стати, Речи, Беседы, Письма.* М: Искусство, 1952.

«Откройте Сезоне в Перой Студии.» *Правда* 219 (1922): 5.

«Отци и Дети. Вторая Студия.» *Зрелища* 59 (1923): 21.

«Первая Студия МХТ.» *Театр и Искусство* 6 (1914): 371.

«Первая Студия МХТ.» *Театр и Студия* 1–2 (1922): 71.

«Первая Студия МХТ.» *Эрмитаж* 5 (1922): 15.

«Первая Студия Художествен. Театр.» *Театр и Музыка* 8 (1922): 68.

«Праздничний Репутуар.» *Известия* 3 (1919): 4.

Прудкин, М. «Страницы Воспоминания.» *Театр* 10 (1983): 101–109.

Рудницкий, К. «Когда Станиславский разговаривал с Вахтанговым о гротеске?» *Вопросы Театра.* М: ВТО, 1970.

Русский Советский Театр 1917–1921. Л: Искусство Ленинград, 1968.

Строева, М. Н. *Режиссёрские Искание Станиславского 1898–1917.* М: Наука, 1973.

_____. «В Чертах гротеска и Русской Сатиры.» *Вопросы Театра.* М: ВТО, 1986.

«Студия.» *Русский Слово* 34 (1914): 7.

«Студия при Худож. Театр.» *Русский Слово* 191 (1913): 6.

«Студия Художественого Театпа.» *Русский Ведомости* 184 (1912): 3.

Таргис, Н. *Театр и Драматургия* Л: 1976.

«Театр им. Евг. Вахтангова» *Программы Гос. Ак. Театров* 26 (1926) 16.

«Театральная Хроника» *Правда* 25 (1922): 5.

Фрейдкина, Л. «У Исторков Формализма в Русском Театре.» *Театр* 6 (1937): 64–82.

_____. «Соблазны и Принципы.» *Театр* 12 (1937): 145–49.

«Хроника.» *Рампа* 10 (1923): 18

«Хроника.» *Рампа и Жизнь* 20 (1916): 7–8.

«Хроника.» *Рампа и Жизнь* 35 (1916): 8.

«Хроника Театра» *Правда* 260 (1919): 3.

«Хроника Театра» *Правда* 237 (1919): 2.

«Четвёртая Студия.» *Новая Рампа* 19 (1924): 13.

«Четвёртая Студия МХТ.» *Театр И Музыка* 11 (1922): 249–250.

Шихматов, Л. «В Третьей Студии.» *Театр* 12 (1962): 120–121.

INDEX